SERIES EDITOR: LEE JOHNSO

OSPREY MILITARY MEN-AT-A

BRITISH FORCES IN NORTH AMERICA
1793-1815

TEXT BY
RENÉ CHARTRAND

COLOUR PLATES BY
GERRY EMBLETON

First published in Great Britain in 1998 by Osprey Publishing
Michelin House, 81 Fulham Road, London SW3 6RB

ISBN 1 85532 741 4

Filmset in Singapore by Pica Ltd
Printed through World Print Ltd., Hong Kong

Editor: Sharon van der Merwe
Designer: Peter Burt

For a catalogue of all titles published by Osprey Military, please write to:
Osprey Marketing, Michelin House, 81 Fulham Road, London SW3 6RB

Acknowledgements

Francis Back, Carl Benn, William Y. Carman, Dennis Carter-Edwards, Brian L. Dunnigan, Bruce Ellis, Paul Fortier, Donald E. Graves, Philip Haythornthwaite, Robert Henderson, Daniel S.C. Mackay, Barry Rich, David Ross, Glenn Steppler, David Webber, the Anne S.K. Brown Military Collection, the Canadian War Museum, the National Historic Sites and Monuments Board of Canada.

Publisher's Note

Readers may wish to study this title in conjunction with some of the many titles in the Men-at-Arms series covering the Napoleonic period in addition to the following Osprey publications:

MAA 39 *British Army in North America 1775-1783*
MAA 226 *The American War 1812-14*
MAA 294 *British Forces in the West Indies 1790-1815*
Elite 48 *Nelson's Navy 1793-1815*
Warrior 20 *British Redcoat (2) 1793-1815*
Campaign 28 *New Orleans 1815*

Artist's Note

Readers may care to note that the original paintings from which the colour plates in this book were prepared are available for private sale. All reproduction copyright whatsoever is retained by the Publisher. All enquiries should be addressed to:

Scorpio Gallery, P.O. Box 475, Hailsham, East Sussex BN27 2SL

The Publishers regret that they can enter into no correspondence upon this matter.

BRITISH FORCES IN NORTH AMERICA 1793-1815

INTRODUCTION

The end of the American Revolution in 1783 confirmed the independence of the republic of the United States of America from Great Britain. Britain, however, still managed to make its presence felt in North America. Several British colonies north of the United States that had not joined the American revolutionaries: Lower Canada (now Quebec), Upper Canada (Ontario), Nova Scotia, New Brunswick, Newfoundland, Prince Edward Island and Cape Breton Island.

The economy of British North America rested on the fur trade, fisheries, agriculture and the relatively new industry of large scale exploitation of forests for wood. This massive source of timber was what made these colonies so attractive to Britain. With the outbreak of the French Revolution and the advent of Napoleon's naval blockade, Britain's traditional European sources of shipbuilding lumber and masts dried up. Increasing shipments from Canada quickly compensated for this shortfall. Large wood rafts were assembled at the new town of Hull, on the Ottawa River, floated down to Quebec City, and loaded and shipped to Britain. Here was a vast supply of wood for the Royal Navy's ships and the world's largest merchant fleet which provided the basic protection of the lifeblood of the island nation. The defence of this all-important geostrategic supply was a powerful motivation in Britain's determination to preserve British North America.

During most of the Napoleonic Wars, North America remained a relatively peaceful area. However, the occasional presence of French fleets, the sale of Louisiana, Indian hostilities against the United States and the impressment of American sailors by the Royal Navy increased tension between the two countries. Britain's Orders in Council concerning trade were a major irritant which, added to the other issues, finally caused the United States to declare war on 19 June 1812. Ironically, the British cabinet had repealed the offensive Orders on 23 June 1812, but it was too late.

American expectations of 'merely marching' into Canada were completely frustrated by the resilient resistance of the small but determined British and Canadian forces. For three years, successive American attempts to invade Canada were repulsed, while British counterattacks eventually gave them control over parts of Michigan and Maine. But when large British forces made efforts to invade northern New York state and lower Louisiana, they were repulsed. Peace was finally proclaimed in early 1815. This North American

The battle of Queenston Heights, fought on 13 October 1812, proved to be a major victory by the British and Canadian forces over the more numerous invading Americans. However, the very talented British General Sir Isaac Brock was killed in the engagement. The surrender of the Americans was received by General Sheaffe as shown in this print by G. Thompson published in Smithfield in December 1812. Brock is shown carried in the left background. (Thompson-Pell Research Centre, Fort Ticonderoga, N.Y.)

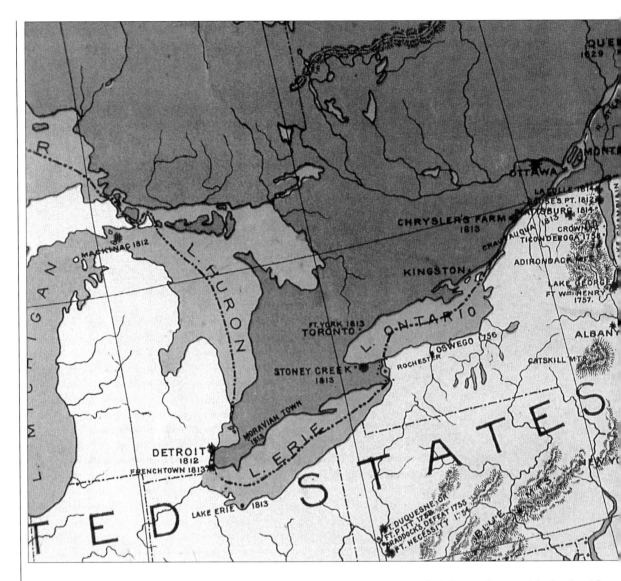

episode of the Napoleonic Wars ended in a draw, with both sides retreating to the pre-1812 borders.[1]

CHRONOLOGICAL TABLE

Abbreviations: AL: Alabama; arty.: Artillery; Bn.: Battalion; Can.: Canadian; co.: company; cos.: companies; det.: detachment; Fenc.: Fencibles; Ft.: Foot; GA: Georgia; IL: Illinois; LA: Louisiana; LC: Lower Canada; LCSEM: Lower Canada Select Embodied Militia; LD: Light Dragoons; LI: Light Infantry; NFLD: Newfoundland; NY: New York; MD: Maryland; ME: Maine; MI: Michigan; OH: Ohio; RA: Royal Artillery; RSM: Royal Sappers & Miners; RM: Royal Marines; RVB: Royal Veterans' Battalion; Tr.: Troop; UC: Upper Canada; VA: Virginia; Vols.: Volunteers; WIR: West India Regiment

---

1 The Indian nations, which were very important in the defence of Canada, cannot be covered in this short book. Readers are referred to MAA 228 *Eastern Woodland Indians*, and an essential study, *His Majesty's Indian Allies*, by Robert S. Allen (Toronto, 1993).

Battlesites of the War of 1812

1791

Canada is divided into the two provinces of Lower Canada (now Quebec) and Upper Canada (now Ontario).

1793

21 January Louis XVI executed; Great Britain, Spain, Holland, Sardinia, Naples and Portugal at war with France.

14 May Surrender of the French islands of St Pierre and Miquelon, south of Newfoundland: 4th Ft.

July to October French fleet anchored at New York; rumours abound that it is to raid Nova Scotia.

1794

20 August Battle of Fallen Timbers between US troops and Indians. Several Loyalist Canadians fighting with the Indians are killed; Americans protest their involvement, contest British garrisons on US territory.

19 November Jay's Treaty signed between United States and Great Britain. All British forts on US territory to be turned over to American forces by 1 June 1796.

1796

French naval squadron raids Grand Banks off Newfoundland.

1801

12 October Cessation of hostilities between Britain and France.

1802

27 March Peace of Amiens between France and England. Spanish Louisiana becomes French.

1803

16 May Britain declares war on France.

30 November Louisiana formally turned over to France and on

20 December is in turn ceded to the United States.

1807

November British Order-in-Council prohibits trade of neutral countries with France and its allies.

1811

May Battle between USS *Guerriere* and HMS *Little Belt*.

7 November Battle of Tippecanoe. Indians under Tecumseh beaten by Americans.

1812

19 June United States declare war on Great Britain.

15 July River Aux Canard, UC: 41st Ft. (1 co.), Militia, Indians.

17 July Fort Michilimackinac (or Mackinac), MI: 10 RVB det., RA, Pothier's Can. Vols., Indians.

9 August Maguago (Brownstown), MI: 41st Ft., 1st Essex Militia, Indians.

15 August Fort Dearborn, Chicago, IL: Indians.

15-16 August Detroit, MI: 41st Ft., 49th Ft., RA, NFLD Fenc. det., 1st York Militia (flank & rifle cos.), 2nd York Militia, 3rd York Militia (flank cos.), 5th Lincoln Militia (1 flank co.), 1st & 2nd Norfolk Militia, 1st Oxford Militia, 1st Essex Militia, Indians.

19 August Odeltown, NY: Indians.

4 September Fort Wayne, Indiana: Indians.

16 September Toussaint Island, UC: NFLD Fenc. det., 1st Grenville Militia.

A private of the 5th Foot, 1792. The regiment served ten years in Canada from 1787. O.M. Spencer, an American who saw officers of the 5th at Fort Niagara in 1794, recalled their 'long scarlet coats faced with light green without any ornament' except silver buttons and 'their hair clubbed'. The men had white lace with a red line. A regimental order book indicates that correct dress was required even in wilderness outposts. Print after E. Dayes. (Anne S. K. Brown Military Collection, Brown University. Photo R. Chartrand)

21 September   Gananoque, UC: 2nd Leeds Militia.

23 September   Prescott, UC: 2nd Grenville Militia.

9 October   Fort Erie, UC: Niagara LD (Merritt's Tr.).

9 October   Near Fort Erie, UC, capture of British brigs HMS *Detroit* and *Caledonia*: 41st Ft. det., NFLD Fenc. det.

13 October   Queenston Heights, UC: RA, 41st Ft., 49th Ft. (flank cos.), Niagara LD (Merritt's Tr.),1st York Militia (1 flank co.), 2nd York Militia (flank cos.), 3rd York Militia (flank cos.), 1st Lincoln Militia (flank cos., arty. & Runchey's Co. of Coloured Men), 2nd, 4th & 5th Lincoln Militia (flank cos.), Indians.

21 October   Gray's Mills (on St Regis Indian Reservation), UC: Indians.

21 November   Bombardment of Fort Niagara, NY: RA (at Fort George UC), 49th Ft., Indians.

23 November   Salmon River, NY: Glengarry LI, Can. Voltigeurs, Royal Montreal Cav., 1st Glengarry & 2nd Grenville Militia.

28 November   Frenchman's Creek, UC (or Black Rock, NY): RA, 41st Ft. (Light co.), 49th Ft., NFLD Fenc. det., 5th Lincoln Militia (1 flank co.), 1st & 2nd Norfolk Militia, Indians.

17-18 December   Mississineway River, Indiana: Indians.

1813

22 January   Frenchtown (or River Raisin), MI: RA, 3 cos. 41st Ft., 10th RVB det., NFLD Fenc. det., 1st Essex Militia, Indians.

7 February   Elizabethtown (or Brockville), UC: 1st Leeds Militia.

22 February   Ogdensburg, NY: RA, 1 co. 8th Ft., NFLD Fenc. det., Glengarry LI, 1st Glengarry Militia, 1st & 2nd Grenville Militia.

27 April   York (now Toronto), UC: RA, 2 cos. 8th Ft., NFLD Fenc. det., Glengarry LI det., UC Incorporated arty., 1st & 3rd York Militia, 1st Lincoln Militia & arty., Indians.

28 April-9 May   Siege of Fort Meigs, OH: RA, 41st Ft., 1st Essex Militia, 1st Kent Militia, Western (or Caldwell's) Rangers, Indians.

5 May   Fort Meigs, OH (capture of Clay's det.): RA, 41st Ft., RM det., NFLD Fenc. det., 1st Essex Militia, Indians.

27 May   Fort George, UC: RA, 8th Ft. det., 49th Ft., NFLD Fenc. det., Glengarry LI det., UC Incorporated Arty. co., 2nd York Militia (flank cos.), Prov. LD (Merritt's Tr.), Runchey's Co. of Coloured Men, Indians.

27 May   Fort Erie, UC: 3rd Lincoln Militia.

29 May   Sackett's Harbor and Stony Point, NY: RA, 5 cos. 8th Ft., 100th Ft. (Grenadier co.), 2 cos. 104th Ft., NFLD Fenc. det., Glengarry LI det., Can. Voltigeurs.

3 June   Isle-aux-Noix, LC, capture of USS *Growler* and *Eagle*: RA,100th Ft. det.; 1st, 2nd, 3rd LCSEM det.

6 June   Stony Creek, UC: RA, 8th Ft., 49th Ft., Prov. LD (Merritt's Tr.)

24 June   Beaver Dams, UC: 8th Ft. (Light co.), 49th Ft., 104th Ft. (flank cos.), Glengarry LI, Can. LD (Coleman's Tr.), Indians.

25 June   Hampton, VA: 102nd Ft., Independent Companies of Foreigners, RM.

4 July   Schlosser, NY: Can. LD (Coleman's Tr.).

11 July   Black Rock (or Frenchman's Creek): NY, raid on US batteries. RA, 8th Ft. det., 41st Ft. det., 49th Ft. det., Can. LD (Coleman's Tr.), 2nd Lincoln Militia (1 flank & arty. cos.), 3rd Lincoln Militia.

31 July   Plattsburg, NY, raided by 1st LCSEM det.

2 August Fort Stephenson, OH. 41st Ft. det., Indians.

10 September Lake Erie naval battle. NFLD Fenc. det. (as marines).

·1 October Near Châteauguay, LC: Can. Voltigeurs det.

5 October Thames River (or Moraviantown), UC: 41st Ft., Can. LD (Coleman's Tr.), Indians.

26 October Châteauguay, LC: Can. Fenc. (Light co.), Can. Voltigeurs (4 cos.), 1st & 3rd LCSEM (Light cos.), Châteauguay Militia (élite co.), 2nd Beauharnois Militia (1 co.), Indians.

10 November Hoople's Creek, UC: 1st Glengarry & 1st Stormont Militia.

11 November Crystler's Farm, UC: RA, 49th Ft., 89th Ft., RM det., Can. Fenc. det., Can. Voltigeurs det., Prov LD (Fraser's Tr.), 1st Stormont Militia, 2nd Grenville Militia, 1st Leeds Militia (Rifle co.), Indians.

13 November Nantcoke Creek, UC: 1st & 2nd Norfolk Militia, 1st Oxford Militia.

12 December Fort George, UC (recaptured by British): 19th LD, 8th Ft., Indians.

15 December McCrae's House, UC: 1st & 2nd Norfolk Militia.

19 December Fort Niagara, NY: RA, 1st Ft., 8th Ft., 41st Ft., UC Incorporated Militia, 2nd Lincoln Militia, Indians.

23 December Eccanachaca (the Holy Ground), AL: Creek Indians.

30 December Black Rock & Buffalo, NY: 19th LD, 1st Ft., 8th Ft., 41st Ft., 89th Ft. (flank cos.), 100th Ft. (flank cos.), Prov. LD (Merritt's Tr.), 2nd & 3rd Lincoln Militia, Indians.

1814

19 February Salmon River, NY: 1st Stormont Militia.

4 March Longwood, UC: 1st Ft. (flank cos.), 89th Ft., 1st Kent Militia (Loyal Kent Vols. co.), Western (or Caldwell's) Rangers.

26 March Missisquoi Bay, LC: Can. Voltigeurs det.

27 March Sehopiska (Horse Shoe Bend), AL: Indians.

30 March LaColle Mills, LC: 13th Ft., 49th Ft., RM det., Can. Voltigeurs det.

31 March Allies enter Paris.

6 April Napoleon abdicates and arrives at Elba on 4 May. War in Europe ends.

5-6 May Oswego, NY: RA, RSM, RM, RM arty., De Watteville, Glengarry LI (McMillan's co.).

14 May Dover (or Cape Vincent), UC: 89th Ft. (Light co.), Can. Voltigeurs det.

26 June Lake Champlain, NY: Can. Voltigeurs det.

28 June Odeltown, LC: Can. Voltigeurs det., Frontier LI.

5 July Chippewa, UC: 19th LD, RA, 1st Ft., 8th Ft., 100th Ft., Western (or Caldwell's) Rangers, Indians.

16 July Sturgeon's Creek (Point au Playe or Turkey Point), UC: 19th LD.

Lt. William Hughes, 39th Foot, c.1810. Hughes, a son of the Barrack Master of Quebec, was one of several Canadians to be commissioned in the British line infantry. The uniform is scarlet, with green collar and lapels, gold buttons, lace, epaulette and belt-plate. Portrait attributed to William von Moll Berczy. (Musée du Québec, Quebec City)

Officer of the 100th Foot, c.1812, wearing a scarlet coat with yellow collar and cuffs, buttoned up lapels, white turnbacks, gold buttons, gold epaulette with silver Prince of Wales feathers, a gilt belt-plate with silver '100' and a crowned badge with silver feathers. The corps was granted the title 'The Prince Regent's County of Dublin Regiment' on 2 May 1812, hence the prince's feathers in the insignia. Silhouette by Buncombe. (National Historic Sites, Parks Canada, Ottawa)

18 July Fort Sullivan, Eastport, ME: RSM.

19 July St David's, UC: 1st Lincoln Militia.

20 July Prairie du Chien, Wisconsin: Michigan Fenc. det., Mississippi Vols., Mississippi Vol. Arty., Pothier's Can. Vols., Green Bay Militia, Indians.

25 July Lundy's Lane, UC: 19th LD, RA, 1st Ft., 8th Ft., 41st Ft. (Light co.), 89th Ft., 100th Ft., 103rd Ft., 104th Ft. (flank cos.), RM arty., Glengarry LI, UC Incorporated Militia, Prov. LD (Merrit's Tr.), 2nd York Militia, 1st, 2nd, 4th & 5th Lincoln Militia, 1st & 2nd Norfolk Militia, 1st Oxford Militia, 1st Middlesex Militia, 1st Essex Militia, Western (or Caldwell's) Rangers, Indians.

1-31 August Fort Erie, UC, siege and assault: 19th LD, RA, RSM, 1st Ft., 8th Ft., 41st Ft., 82nd Ft., 89th Ft., 100th Ft., 103rd Ft., 104th Ft. (flank cos.), Glengarry LI, Indians.

4 August Ft. Michilimackinac (or Mackinac), MI: NFLD Fenc. det., Glengarry LI det., Michigan Fenc., Pothier's Can. Vols., Indians.

24 August Bladensburg, MD & Washington: RA, RSM, 4th Ft., 21st Ft., 44th Ft., 85th Ft., RM, RM arty.

1 September Castine, ME: RA, RSM, 29th Ft., 60th Ft. (7th Bn. Rifles, two cos.), 62nd Ft., 98th Ft.

3 September Hampden, ME: RA, RSM, flank cos. of 29th Ft., 62nd Ft., 98th Ft..

3 September Bangor, ME: 29th Ft. (Bn. cos.), 60th Ft. (7th Bn. Rifles, 1 co.).

3 September Capture of USS *Tigress*: NFLD Fenc. det., Indians.

September Fort Erie, UC (during September, exclusive of the sortie and action of 17 September): 19th LD, RA, RSM, 1st Ft., 6th Ft., 8th Ft., 82nd Ft., 89th Ft., Glengarry LI, UC Incorporated Militia.

6 September Capture of USS *Scorpion*: NFLD Fenc. det., Indians.

6-11 September Plattsburg, NY: 19th LD (2 squads), RA, RSM, 3rd Ft., 5th Ft., 8th Ft. (2nd Bn.), 13th Ft., 16th Ft., 27th Ft. (1st & 3rd bns.), 39th Ft., 58th Ft., 76th Ft., 88th Ft., De Meuron, Can. Voltigeurs, Can. Chasseurs, 3rd LCSEM.

12 September North Point, MD: RA, 4th Ft., 21st Ft., 44th Ft. 85th Ft., RM, RM arty.

13 September Fort McHenry, MD: RA, RSM, 4th Ft., 21st Ft., 44th Ft., 85th Ft., RM, RM arty.

13 September Machias, ME: 29th Ft., 60th Ft. (1 co. 7th Bn. Rifles)

15 September Fort Bowyer, AL: RM.

17 September Fort Erie, UC, sortie of: 19th LD, RA, 1st Ft., 6th Ft., 8th Ft., 82nd Ft., 89th Ft., 97th Ft., Glengarry LI.

15 October Chippewa, UC: 2nd Lincoln Militia.

19 October Cook's Mills (on Lyon's Creek), UC: 1st Ft., Glengarry LI, Indians.

6 November Malcolm's Mills, UC: 1st & 2nd Norfolk Militia, 1st Oxford Militia, 1st Middlesex Militia, Indians.

14 December Lake Borgne, LA: RM, sailors.

23 December Near Velere's Plantation, 7 miles below New Orleans, LA: RA, RSM, 4th Ft., 21st Ft., 44th Ft., 85th Ft., 95th Rifles.

24 December Treaty of Ghent ends the war between Britain and the United States, but it takes several weeks for the news to reach North America.

1815

8-9 January New Orleans, LA: RA, RSM, R Staff Corps, 14th LD (two dismounted squadrons), 4th Ft., 7th Ft., 21st Ft., 27th Ft. (1st Bn.), 40th Ft., 43rd Ft., 44th Ft., 85th Ft., 93rd Ft., 95th Rifles, RM, RM arty., 1 WIR, 5 WIR.

13 January Point Petre, GA: RM, RM arty., 2 WIR det., Royal West India Rangers det.

11 February Fort Bowyer, AL: RA, RSM, 4th Ft., 21st Ft., 40th Ft., 44th Ft., RM, RM arty.

THE BRITISH REGULAR ARMY

Miniature of Lt. Daniel Claus, 49th Foot, c.1812, wearing a scarlet coatee with green collar and lapels, gold buttons, epaulettes and lace. Officers' coat buttonholes were stitched through on both sides. Lt. Claus was killed at the battle of Chrysler's Farm in November 1813. He was a Canadian, and the son of Sir William Claus of the Indian Department. (National Archives of Canada, C19120)

In spite of fairly numerous and reasonably effective militias, the backbone of the defence of British North America remained the British regular regiments posted to the various colonies. With Britain embroiled in its long struggle against France elsewhere in the world, the number of regulars posted to North America was very moderate. Two regiments were posted in Canada for an exceptionally long time, the 41st Foot from 1799 to 1815, and the 49th Foot from 1802 to 1815. They gave outstanding service during the War of 1812 against the Americans, possibly because of increased familiarity with the country and its peoples. While there were some reinforcements in 1813, it was not really until 1814, once the war in Europe had ended, that tens of thousands of men, mostly from Wellington's army in France, were sent to North America.

The following corps served in North America between 1793 and 1815: 14th Light Dragoons (Louisiana 1815); 19th Light Dragoons (Canada 1813-1816); Royal Artillery (all colonies 1793-1815); Royal Engineers (all colonies 1793-1815); Royal Military Artificers/Royal Sappers and Miners (Nova Scotia, Prince Edward Island, New Brunswick 1794-1815, Newfoundland 1807-1815, Canada 1813-1815, American coast & Louisiana 1814-1815); Royal Staff Corps (Nova Scotia 1814-15); 1st Foot (Canada 1812-1815); 3rd Foot (Canada 1814-1815); 4th Foot (Nova Scotia 1787-1794, Canada 1794-1797, Bermuda, American coast & Louisiana 1814-1815); 5th Foot (Canada 1787-1797, 1814-1815); 6th Foot (Canada 1799-1806, 1814-1815); 7th Foot (Canada 1791-1794, Nova Scotia 1794-1802, 1808-1810, Louisiana 1815); 8th Foot (1st Bn. Canada 1809-1815, 2nd Bn. Nova Scotia & New Brunswick 1810-1814, Canada 1814-1815); 9th Foot (Canada 1814-1815); 13th Foot (Canada 1813-1815); 16th Foot (Canada 1814-1815); 21st Foot (American coast & Louisiana 1814-1815); 23rd Foot (Nova Scotia 1808-1810); 24th Foot (Canada 1789-1799, Nova Scotia 1799-1800); 26th Foot (Canada 1787-1800, 1814-1815); 27th Foot (Canada 1814-1815); 29th Foot (Nova Scotia 1802-1807, Maine 1814-1815); 37th Foot (Canada 1814-1815); 39th Foot (Canada 1814-1815); 40th Foot (Louisiana 1815); 41st Foot (Canada 1799-1815); 43rd Foot (Louisiana 1815); 44th Foot (American coast & Louisiana 1814-1815); 49th Foot (Canada 1802-1815); 57th Foot (Canada 1814-1815); 58th Foot (Canada 1814-1815); 60th Foot (Canada and Nova Scotia 1786-1803, 5th Bn. Nova Scotia 1803-1805, 7th Bn. Nova Scotia & Maine 1814-1817); 62nd Foot (Nova Scotia, Prince Edward Island & Bermuda 1814-1827); 64th Foot (Nova Scotia 1813-1815); 66th

Brass belt-plates of the 104th Foot, 93rd Foot and 44th Foot, c.1812-1815. (Mr. and Mrs. Don Troiani collection, Southbury, CT)

Foot (Nova Scotia 1799-1800, Newfoundland 1800-1802); 70th Foot (Canada 1813-1827); 76th Foot (Canada 1814-1827); 81st Foot (Canada 1814-1815); 82nd Foot (Canada 1814-1815); 85th Foot (Bermuda & American coast 1814-1815); 88th Foot (Canada 1814-1815); 89th Foot (Nova Scotia 1812-1813, Canada 1813-1815); 90th Foot (Canada 1814-1815), 93rd Foot (2nd Bn. Newfoundland 1814-1815, 1st Bn. Louisiana 1815); 95th Rifles (Louisiana 1814-1815); 97th Foot (Canada 1814-1815); 98th Foot (Nova Scotia 1805-1815); 99th Foot (Nova Scotia 1806-1818); 100th Foot (Nova Scotia 1805-1807, Canada 1807-1818); 101st Foot (Canada 1813-1814); 102nd Foot (Bermuda & American coast 1813-1815, Canada 1815-1818); 103rd Foot (Canada 1812-1817); 104th Foot (New Brunswick 1810-1813, Canada 1813-1817); 10th Royal Veterans Bn. (Canada & Nova Scotia 1807-1815); De Meuron (Canada 1813-1816); De Watteville (Canada 1813-1816); Royal Marines (American coast, Bermuda & Canada 1813-1814, Louisiana and Alabama 1814-1815); Royal Marine Artillery (American Coast, Bermuda & Canada 1813-1816, Louisiana and Alabama 1814-1815).

BRITISH ARMY DRESS

In general, the uniforms worn by the enlisted men of British Army units in North America were practically identical to those worn in Europe. In the 1790s, they wore white breeches, long gaiters and bicorn hats. The long-tailed coats with lapels were replaced after 1797 by single-breasted coatees.

From 1800, stovepipe shakos were issued. They were worn until the new 'Belgic' shakos, announced in Quebec General Orders on 3 August 1812, were received with the 1813 clothing issue; shakos were issued every second year, so some regiments did not receive theirs until 1814. Not all issues went according to plan, however, perhaps the most unusual being the white tropical shakos sent to the 13th Foot, although these were replaced by black ones in August 1813. By 1814, all units should have had the 'Belgic' shako.

Before 1812, white breeches and black knee-length gaiters were the official dress. These were replaced by grey pantaloons from 1812, although some regiments, such as the 49th Foot, had grey pantaloons and 'leggings' made in Canada in September 1811. By 1813 most regiments had grey pantaloons and grey short gaiters, although white breeches had already been forwarded 'for several Regiments serving in Canada' for 1813. The 99th Foot was thus issued white breeches and long gaiters for that year. White breeches were also sent to the flank companies of the 100th Foot in December 1812 for their 1813 issue.

Only one Highland regiment, the 93rd, served in North America during this period. The 1st Battalion was part of the doomed assault against the American lines at New Orleans in January 1815. Anticipating an arduous campaign, the government tartan cloth was used to make trews and the blue undress bonnet instead of kilts. With an unusually high red and white diced band, the bonnet was worn at New Orleans instead of the feather bonnet. The 2nd Battalion was in Newfoundland during 1814-15 and apparently wore the usual kilt and dress bonnet.

Army officers in North America were required to obtain the same new pattern uniforms as Europe. This basically meant the long-tailed coat with white breeches and a bicorn hat. But there was an interlude from 1 July 1800 until 1806 when a black round hat with a fur crest was ordered worn in ordinary duties by officers in British North America. A garrison order in Halifax mentions that officers were now to wear bicorn hats instead, and to wear gaiters instead of boots.

From early 1812, the new 'Belgic' shako, the short-tailed coatee, grey pantaloons and short boots were to be worn by officers. Clothiers in Montreal and Quebec imported the necessary items of dress and advertised in the newspapers so that officers could purchase the items in Canada. In September 1812, the new 'Military Officer's Regulation beaver caps [shako], trimmed with rich gold chains, Bullion tassels, Gilt plate and Feather' were already on sale in Montreal. In October 1812 the officers of 103rd Foot were dressed in Belgic shakos, coatees and pantaloons 'of the new Pattern and in conformity with His Majesty's Regulations', but uniform issues had not yet caught up with the enlisted men, who had 'much worn' older uniforms.

In the 104th Foot, the new uniform was first seen in July 1812 when several new officers arrived at St John (New Brunswick) from England, their novel appearance causing some amusement. One of these officers, Capt. Le Couteur, commented on the grey overalls with buttons as a 'vile dress for service, too tight for a run so that we soon got to grey trowzers'. He further reported that the 'neat Hessian boot and tight pantaloons, the most dressy of all uniforms, was the evening or full dress'.

However, one could also find plenty of officers in uniforms 'not conformable' to the new regulations during 1812. The officers of the 1st Battalion., 1st Foot (Royal Scots), recently arrived from the West Indies, were inspected at Quebec in September 1812 wearing round hats and white linen pantaloons with half boots. Nor did one have to come from the West Indies to enjoy the comfort of round hats. At the battle of Queenston Heights in October 1812, all British officers, from generals to subalterns, were said to be wearing them. Meanwhile, in Halifax, officers of the 2nd Battalion., 8th Foot, still had white breeches, and the 98th Foot's officers wore the pre-1812 uniform. But officers tried to conform to the changes. In September 1812, Lt. Nowland of the 100th Foot, who were encamped at Blairfindie in Lower Canada, asked his wife to have 'overalls' made for him as all were 'ordered to wear them'. By 1813, one can safely assume that most British officers in Canada had the new order of dress.

In May 1813, three squadrons of the 19th Light Dragoons arrived in Canada. An inspection of the two squadrons left in Radipole, Ireland, in October 1813 reports its uniform was still 'according to [the] old pattern', which was the Tarleton helmet, the blue dolman with yellow collar and cuffs, and white (silver for officers) buttons and cords. The new Light Dragoon

British infantryman, probably drawn in Québec, c.1813-1816. In spite of its crudeness, this illustration shows interesting details. The Belgic shako has the brass plate and white cords, but a red over white plume instead of having red at the base. The coatee is red with dark blue collar and cuffs, and white turnbacks; white lace not only trims the buttonholes, but edges the front and the top of the cuffs – a detail sometimes seen in British prints. Trousers are grey, gaiters are black, and the knapsack is of the French type with fur rather than the usual box-like 'Trotter' model. Accoutrements are white with a square brass belt-plate. The sentry box is grey. The white paint used on this drawing for the lace, cords and turnbacks has turned to grey. (Archives nationales du Québec, Iconog. A10.4-FP10.2)

uniform with shako and coatee with lapels was sent to Canada for issue in December 1813. The officer's lace, ordered changed from silver to gold in 1812 with the new uniform, was actually changed from 1814.

For details of the regimental uniforms of British regulars, see *Wellington's Infantry* (MAA 114, MAA 119), *Wellington's Light Cavalry* (MAA 126), and *Wellington's Specialist Troops* (MAA 204).

WINTER DRESS IN CANADA

The severe winter weather in Canada demanded effective ways to keep warm and comfortable. Initially, British soldiers wore the *capot*, a winter coat used by the French Canadian population. Also occasionally called a 'blanket coat' as it was often made from thick blankets, this garment was full skirted and had a hood. A wool or fur cap was worn with the capot, and footwear was moccasins, with metal 'creepers' attached when the ground was icy. By the 1790s, however, there was a desire to wear something more 'military'.

On 23 April 1801, a royal warrant directed that 'each man of our regiments of Foot Guards and Infantry of the Line' would forthwith be furnished with a regulation greatcoat issued from 25 December 1802. It was described in the 1802 Regulations 'to be of a dark Grey Woolen Stuff Kersey wove, loose made, to come well up about the Neck, have a large Falling Cape to cover the Shoulders, and they are to reach down to the Calf of the Leg, as per Pattern Great Coat...' It was double breasted and the cape worn over the shoulders was removable. Sergeants were allowed to have cuffs and collars in the regimental facing colour. Wearers in Canada complained that it wore out fast and was not warm enough. In 1811, the men's greatcoats for North America were ordered to be made warmer and also to be issued every two years instead of every three years.

In the autumn and early spring, shakos, shoes and other garments would be worn as in Europe, but in winter, fur caps, mitts and winter 'Beef Boots' were worn. A District General Order given at Montreal on 11 December 1814 mentioned that 'The Beef Shoes are not to be worn over the Common Shoes, the Men's feet are to be well wrapt up, in some woollen stuff and the Beef Shoes then drawn over the wrappers' (C687). The fur cap could be quite stylish.

Officer's winter dress originally included capots, but with the arrival of changing fashions in the 1790s, a blue greatcoat became the proper dress for the fashionable officer in winter. The regulations concerning the dress of British officers in North America recognised it in the General Orders of 1 July 1800:

'The Great Coats of the Officers are invariably to be made of blue cloth double breasted with Regimental Buttons and edged throughout with the colour of the lappel of the Regiment, those only excepted whose lappels are blue and the edging of whose Great Coats will therefore be scarlet. The Sword and Sashes are always to be worn outside and the Gorget of Officers for duty suspended from the upper buttons of the lappels...they are to wear over hose [overalls] of pepper and salt [grey] coloured Cloth or Kerseymere with the Regimental Buttons strapped with black leather and covered at the bottom also with black leather so as to shew similar to an half boot.' (C223)

Capt. Guy C. Colgough, Grenadier Company, 103rd Foot, c.1814. He wears a scarlet coatee with a pale buff collar edged scarlet at the front and top, pale buff piping edging the buttoned up lapel, gold buttons and gold wings on scarlet. The *Army List* gives the facings as white for the 103rd, but they were actually buff as shown in this portrait, as well as in C. Hamilton Smith's charts and uniform orders to the tailors Hawkes and Buckmaster. (Château de Ramezay Museum, Montreal)

In the coldest part of winter, 'large fur caps' and 'immense tippets of fur round their neck' would be worn by dandy young officers in Quebec City. In Halifax, Lt. Thomas Henry Browne of the 23rd Fusiliers described the officers being 'closely wrapped up in great coats lined with fur, and fox skin caps on our head' in 1808. On 24 December 1811, a general order to the whole army specified that the greatcoats be grey. In effect, officers were ordered to wear greatcoats similar to those of the men.

As for cavalry, only the 19th Light Dragoons served in Canada from 1813 to 1816. Cavalrymen had long cloaks and the 19th soon found that theirs were not quite up to a Canadian winter. Their dark blue cloaks were transformed 'into coats with sleeves' since the accoutrements had to be worn constantly over the coats in the 'peculiar climate' of Canada.

COLONIAL REGULAR UNITS

Following the end of the American War of Independence, there were no colonial regular troops in British North America but, as the settlement of Upper Canada expanded westward, the need for such a force was felt. In 1791, the Queen's Rangers were authorised for service in Upper Canada. Two years later, Great Britain and its empire was at war with France which caused the withdrawal of some British regiments towards Europe and the West Indies. However, the presence of French warships in the North Atlantic and tensions with the United States led to the formation of additional regular colonial units to bolster the remaining British regulars. Most of the officers were native or residents of North America. In 1798, the units were given the status of fencibles for service in North America. Except for the Queen's Rangers, the colonial regular units listed below did not appear in the *Army List* and thus have remained almost completely unknown. All were disbanded in 1802, following the news of peace with France. Renewed war with France in 1803 meant raising new colonial fencible regiments for service in British North America. This time, the regiments were raised within the British establishment and so appeared in the *Army List*. The officers were usually from Britain.

The **Queen's Rangers**, authorised formed from 20 December 1791 on the British establishment for service in the new province of Upper Canada, were to have 432 all ranks in two companies, but actual strength hovered around 300 men. The colonel was John Graves Simcoe, the celebrated commander of the élite Loyalist Queen's Rangers during the American Revolution, who was now also lieutenant-governor of Upper Canada. The corps was formed in 1792 following the arrival of the recruits from England at Quebec on 27 May. The new unit, partly recruited from Loyalist veterans, was dressed as

Brass shako plate, 41st Foot, c.1814-1815. (National Historic Sites, Parks Canada, Ottawa)

Gustavus Nicolls, Royal Engineers, c.1815. He wears a scarlet coat with blue collar, lapels (and cuffs), gold epaulettes, lace and buttons, a crimson sash, and a bicorn with a white plume barely visible at lower right. Nicolls served in North America, taking part in the British expeditions in Maine during 1814. He later designed the citadel at Halifax, Nova Scotia. (Halifax Citadel National Historic Site)

Private of the 6th Regiment of Foot in winter dress, Canada, c.1806. The fur cap has a peak, a white "6" on a red background, and a white over red tuft. The cape of the double-breasted grey greatcoat has been removed. Water-colour by Cecil C.P. Lawson after an original in the Library of Windsor Castle. (Anne S. K. Brown Military Collection, Brown University. Photo R. Chartrand)

light infantry, but actually served more as a garrison and pioneer corps. It was posted mainly at Fort George, York (Toronto) and Fort St Joseph, and was disbanded in October 1802.

The first uniform was to be 'in green with a blue Cuff, and Collar, bordered with White Lace, according to the Pattern herewith enclosed' (now lost) on 18 November 1791 (WO 3/10). However, the blue facings were soon changed to black. From about 1798, the cut of the men's coatee is shown by C.H. Smith as similar to that of the line, but in green instead of red. The breeches were probably white, gaiters black and 'green cloth trowsers' were also issued.

The first headgear, issued in late 1791 or early 1792, was 'a thin leather cap', apparently the same as that of the Queen's Rangers during the American Revolution (black with a white metal crescent). From 1793, a 'leather light infantry cap', shown as an early shako by C.H. Smith, was worn with a green plume, and possibly a brass bugle badge. The clothing was often issued in arrears, with many men being owed three years' issues when the corps was disbanded. The men were armed as line infantry with muskets and bayonets, the sergeants with halberds and swords. Accoutrements are shown white. The officers had uniforms of the same cut as line officers but in the corps colours of green faced black with silver buttons, epaulettes and lace. Their buttonhole lace was of a unique wavy pattern ending in a point.

Authorised on 8 February 1793, the **Royal Nova Scotia Regiment** with an establishment of 800 men raised from April, had an effective strength of 600. There were detachments at St John's, Newfoundland, and Cape Breton Island from 1794, but most of the regiment was garrisoned at Halifax where it was disbanded on 24 August 1802.

Uniform was to be red faced blue, but in 1793, before the regular clothing arrived from England, the regiment had brown jackets, white trousers, brown caps, shoes, shirts, buckles and stocks. By early 1794, blue trousers were also reported. Meanwhile, part of the regiment's clothing was captured by a French privateer, while some that did arrive was 'thin coarse sleezy stuff fit only for the West Indies'. The pouches proved to be for cavalry and had to be returned. By May 1794, blue jackets were procured 'there being no red cloth in town' (CO 217/76). With all these difficulties, the regiment was nicknamed 'Sans culottes' by Halifax wags, but finally obtained its captured red faced blue clothing in 1795 by purchasing it in Boston. The waistcoat and breeches were white, with bicorn hats for fusiliers and grenadiers, red waistcoats, 'light infantry' caps for the light company, and grey pantaloons according to a 1797 list. The coatee without lapels was possibly part of the 1799 issue, and a surviving example of this rare garment has a plain white lace square-ended and set in pairs. By July 1801, the colonel complained that clothing had not been received for two years. As the regiment was disbanded in 1802, it probably never had the stovepipe shako. The officer's lace and buttons were gold.

The **King's New Brunswick Regiment** was raised from 25 April 1793, with an establishment of 600 men and effective strength of about 300 men in six companies. Most were stationed at Fredericton, with detachments at St John or St Andrew's. It was disbanded in September 1802.

Uniform was first issued in 1793 with 'a short blue jacket with Scarlet cuff and cape [collar], flannel under the waistcoat with sleeves, Brown cloth trousers and round Hatt' (CO 188/7). Later issues were red faced blue, probably with white lace, white waistcoat and breeches. There were 'Caps' for light infantry and grenadier companies, and bicorn hats for fusiliers until they were replaced by the stovepipe shako in 1801.

Authorised on 5 February 1794, the **Island of St John's Volunteers** was to have 200 men in two companies, but actual strength was about half the establishment. Recruited from May 1794 on the Island of St John (renamed Prince Edward Island in 1800) and stationed at Charlottetown, the regiment's name was changed to H.M. Prince Edward Island Fencibles in 1800. The corps was disbanded in August 1802.

Uniforms were red faced green, with white lace, white waistcoat and breeches, and a bicorn hat. No new clothing was sent and, in 1797, the corps resorted to wearing blue jackets with red cuffs and collar, blue pantaloons in winter and 'white linen Trowsers in the Summer with Caps cut after a fancy Pattern of our own'. For fatigues, the men had 'small round hats ... and any old rag they could put on' (MG 24, F1, 2). The officers had gold buttons and epaulettes. A surviving officers' coat has the collar, cuffs and lapels piped white.

The **Royal Canadian Volunteers** were raised during 1794 and recruited from 1795, with two battalions of 750 men each in ten companies; actual strength hovered at about 430 per battalion. The officers and men of the 1st Battalion were recruited among French Canadians in Lower Canada and served in Montreal and Quebec City. The 2nd Battalion was recruited mostly from English Canadians with some French Canadians, and served in Upper Canada. There were tensions with the Americans for the 2nd Battalion at Fort George, Fort Malden and Fort St Joseph in Upper Canada, but no violent incidents. This regiment, the first to embody French and English Canadians for regular service, was disbanded during August 1802.

Uniform was red faced blue, with white lace with a red and a yellow line for the men. The coats had long tails with white turnbacks until 1800, and were short-tailed coatees later. The blue lapels seem to have been worn throughout. The waistcoat was red rather than white, there were white breeches and black gaiters for dress and grey trousers (apparently gaiter-trousers) changed to blue in 1800. Round hats were worn for undress. Otherwise, headgear was a black bicorn edged with white lace, with a white-over-red plume, until replaced by the stovepipe shako from 1801 for fusiliers. Grenadiers had bearskin caps and light infantry had 'caps with bugles and green feathers', which were probably early shakos with brass bugle badges (C792). The officers had gold buttons and lace set in pairs, white waistcoat and breeches, and unlaced bicorn hats. The Royal Canadian Volunteers had brown greatcoats in 1796, followed by grey ones four years later, worn with fur caps, mitts, and grey trousers.

'An Officer of the British Army and a Merchant of Quebec in their Winter Dress' in 1807 from John Lambert's *Travels*. The officer (left) wears the 1800 regulation dark blue greatcoat with a fur cap in the shape of a shako, boots, mitts and a fur tippet. (National Archives of Canada, C113668)

Authorised raised on 12 April 1795 with an establishment of 600 men recruited in Newfoundland, the **Royal Newfoundland Regiment** served there until April 1800 when eight companies were transferred to Halifax, with two companies remaining at St John's. It was disbanded on 31 July 1802.

Uniforms were red faced blue, with plain white lace for the men. The officer's lace was probably gold.

The **Royal Newfoundland Fencibles** were authorised raised on 6 June 1803 for service in North America. They were to have an establishment of 1,000 men recruited in Newfoundland, but had 536 all ranks when war broke out in 1812. They gained the prefix 'Royal' on 17 October 1803. Transferred to first Nova Scotia in 1806, then to Quebec City in 1811, a detachment of five companies was sent to Upper Canada in the summer of 1812 to serve as marines on the British ships on the Great Lakes. This unit was engaged in many actions. The remaining 348 all ranks were sent back to St John's, Newfoundland, in September 1815 and disbanded on 24 June 1816.

They wore red coatees with blue facings; men's lace was white with two red lines between a blue central line made square-ended and set at equal space. Officers had gold buttons and epaulettes.

The **Nova Scotia Fencibles** were authorised raised on 9 July 1803 for service in Nova Scotia where it was recruited. The headquarters was first in Halifax, then in Annapolis, with detachments in various localities. Transferred to Newfoundland in June 1805, sent to Quebec City in July 1814 and on to Kingston (Upper Canada) in August, the regiment did not have the opportunity to be in action. In June 1816, the regiment went back to Nova Scotia and was disbanded at Halifax on 24 July 1816.

The uniform consisted of a red coatee with yellow facings; men's lace was white with a yellow line and a black line made bastion-ended and set at an equal space. Officers had silver buttons and epaulettes. A c.1810 tailor's note mentions that the officer's coat was cut the same way as the 91st, with buttons set in pairs, two at each end of the collar and 'Breast Button for skirt ornament'. The regimental insignia was the coat of arms of the colony of Nova Scotia. It was worn on the buttons and belt-plates and also, by permission since 1804, on the shako plate. Permission had further been granted for the officers to wear shakos rather than hats on 28 May 1804.

Authorised raised on 1 August 1803 for service in New Brunswick, the **New Brunswick Fencibles** (104th Foot) were also recruited, from Nova Scotia and Lower Canada. There were nearly 700 officers and men in 1806. Although the companies had buglers instead of drummers, the regimental band still had drums. The pioneers of the regiment were negroes, as was the band's bass drummer.

Lt. Col. David Shank, Queen's Rangers, c.1798. Shank commanded the corps from 1796 to 1798. His uniform consists of a dark green coat with a black velvet collar and lapels open below the neck, silver buttons and epaulettes; note the wavy pointed silver lace and crimson sash. (Print after portrait)

As the regiment volunteered to serve anywhere in the world with the British Army, its status changed from fencible to a regiment of the line infantry numbered 104th in 1810. It retained, however, the title of New Brunswick Regiment. In spite of this change in status, the regiment remained posted in southern New Brunswick. When troops were urgently needed to boost the few regulars in Canada, six companies made an extraordinary winter march of hundreds of kilometres across the frozen wilderness from Fredericton to Quebec City in February and March of 1813. Two other companies were sent from St John, New Brunswick, by sea in May. The 104th then marched to Upper Canada where it distinguished itself in many engagements. The two remaining companies detached at Sydney, Cape Breton Island, and Charlottetown, Prince Edward Island, joined the regiment in Upper Canada in the autumn of 1814. Transferred to Quebec City in August 1815, and to Montreal a year later, it was disbanded in Montreal on 24 May 1817.

The regiment wore a red coatee with pale buff facings. The men's lace was white with a buff central line between a blue and a red line made square-ended and set in pairs. A surviving coatee shows the buff facings to have been made with white material. Officers had silver buttons and epaulettes. An existing officer's coatee has light buff facings, the buttonholes being unlaced. The regimental insignia, worn on the buttons and belt-plates, bore the name of the regiment and the number '104' after 1810.

The **Canadian Fencibles** were authorised raised on 8 August 1803 for service in Lower Canada. Part of the regiment was initially recruited in Scotland, but the Scottish recruits mutinied at Glasgow before departing for North America in 1804. The regiment was eventually recruited to about 700 men mostly from among the French Canadian population of Lower Canada. It was usually posted in the area south of Montreal; a detachment was sent to Fort Malden (Upper Canada) and Detroit in September 1812, another detachment to York (Toronto). Most of the regiment was in eastern Upper Canada in 1813. Various companies were in engagements in Upper and Lower Canada. It was disbanded at Montreal in June 1816.

The uniform was a red coatee with yellow facings; men's lace was white with two blue lines made square-ended and set at equal space according to C.H. Smith. However, Pearse's notes for making uniforms for the Canadian Fencibles indicates that the men's lace was to be set in pairs. Officers had gold buttons and epaulettes. The regimental insignia was a crowned Scots thistle on the buttons and belt-plates, probably because the regiment was originally intended to be recruited in Scotland.

Authorised raised on 13 February 1812 by local order of Sir George Prevost, the **Glengarry Light Infantry** were to have been recruited from the Glengarry Scottish settlers in eastern Upper Canada but eventually this extended to Lower Canada and New Brunswick. Recruiting went smoothly and the initial establishment of 400 men was raised to 600 in May and 800 in August. Placed on the British establishment in August, they were first posted to Trois-Rivières (Lower Canada) for training, and transferred to Upper Canada in October 1812. The regiment was engaged in many actions in Upper Canada during the war, and dissolved at Kingston on 24 June 1816.

TOP **Flank company private's coatee, Royal Nova Scotia Regiment, c.1798-1802. Red with blue collar, cuffs, shoulder straps and wings, white turnbacks, white lace, pewter buttons. (The Army Museum, Halifax Citadel)**

ABOVE **Coat of Capt. John MacDonald, Island of St John's Volunteers, c.1797-1802: scarlet with green collar, cuffs and lapels, white piping and turnbacks, and gold buttons. The coat, apparently locally made, was cut for a big man, which justifies MacDonald's nickname in Gaelic: Ian Moor, or Big John. (Garden of the Gulf Museum, Montague, Prince Edward Island)**

Initially, a Highland uniform of red faced white with Glengarry tartan plaid was proposed, but this was rejected in favour of the dress of the 95th Rifles. Until the green regimental uniform was made and issued, the corps had an undress uniform of 'white cloth Jackets with green cuff and cape [collar] and green foraging caps' at Trois-Rivières during the summer of 1812 (C1218). The men's regimental uniform was a 'bottle green' jacket with black collar, cuffs and shoulder straps piped white; there were 'three rows of white metal bell buttons' according to a veteran of the unit, Jonathan Phillips, and green pantaloons, a 'bucket-shaped' shako with a green plume, and bugle badge with 'GLI' between the strings. In winter, Phillips recalled, 'we wore fur caps, with a long green cloth hanging from the top over the left shoulder, and at the end of this green cloth a green tassel'. The regiment had its muskets fitted with sights. The accoutrements were black.

The officers had a green dolman with black velvet collar and cuffs, black mohair cords, three rows of plain silver ball buttons, green pantaloons, black shako with green plume and silver bugle badge with 'GLI'. The crimson sash is said to have been worn Scottish style over the shoulder, a fashion shown on the portrait of Capt. Roxburgh. However, the portraits of Lt. Col. Macdonnel and Capt. Gugy do not show the sash over the shoulder, so it must have also been worn at the waist, Macdonnel is shown with a green pelisse with black cords and edged with black fur. They wore black pouches and belts, with a silver whistle and chain, and a green and silver sabre knot. It was all very 'conformable to the King's regulations' according to the regiment's July 1815 inspection report (WO 27/133).

Following the transfer of the 104th from New Brunswick to Upper Canada, the colony hardly had any regular troops. In October 1812, a new regiment of **New Brunswick Fencibles**, to be 650 strong, was authorised on the British establishment to be recruited and to serve in the colony. It was to have light infantry muskets, and bugles instead of drums. This news was received in New Brunswick during February 1813, but less than 400 men were eventually recruited. It served in various garrisons in the province and on coastal gunboats. The regiment did not see action and was disbanded on 24 February 1816.

Orders in October 1812 instructed that the uniform was to be the same as the previous New Brunswick Fencibles (104th Foot), but C.H. Smith gives the facings as light yellow, with a plain white lace square-ended and set at equal space. This was possibly the 'Pattern Facing and Looping' approved by the Prince Regent in April 1814. However, it was never worn, as the new unit received no clothing from England. Instead, part of the uniform supply already in the colony intended for the New Brunswick militia (see below) was issued to the regiment. This probably consisted of the red coatees with white collar, cuffs and shoulder straps, and white lace. The accoutrements were probably the black ones from militia stores. The officer's uniform was probably scarlet faced light buff, with silver buttons and epaulettes.

The **Independent Companies of Foreigners** were also known as the 'French Independent Companies' because they were recruited from French deserters including officers. The first company of 100 men was organised in England from September 1812, and the second company from January 1813. Intended for the West Indies, the first company was

Capt. Louis C.H. Fromenteau, Royal Canadian Volunteers, 1st Battalion, 1800. He wears a scarlet coat with dark blue collar and lapels piped white, gilt buttons, epaulettes and belt-plate. Miniature on paper by an unknown artist. (National Archives of Canada, C125655)

Lt. Otto Schwartz, Nova Scotia Fencibles, c.1806, wearing a scarlet coat with yellow collar and lapels, silver buttons and epaulettes; white belt and silver belt-plate bearing the crowned arms of Nova Scotia, and a crimson sash. (Print after silhouette by Charles Buncombe)

Brass belt-plate of the Royal Newfoundland Fencibles Regiment, c.1803-1816. (Niagara Historical Society Museum, Niagara-on-the-Lake, Ont.)

A wooden drum of the Nova Scotia Fencibles, c.1804-1816. This unit was permitted to bear the coat of arms of its province of origin in 1804 and they are shown, partly worn away, with supporters and flags on a yellow background. (Canadian War Museum, Ottawa)

sent to Bermuda instead in early 1813, and was noted for its bad discipline. They embarked with Sir Sydney Beckwick's force, which included the second company, to raid the American coast. On 25 June, the force landed at Hampton, VA, where they met with some resistance, the Americans apparently massacring 17 men trapped in a stranded boat. The foreigners went on the rampage, looting the town, raping women and murdering an 'aged inhabitant' in his bed. Sent back on board ship, they were termed 'an open banditti, who it is impossible to control'. They were shipped to Halifax where they misbehaved as soon as they landed. After four days, the governor reported, 'The inhabitants of Halifax are in the greatest alarm about these fellows', but it seems that the disappearance of some of the men's pay was a cause of unrest. Stricter discipline was imposed but they were sent back to England in September 1813, and disbanded in early May 1814.[2]

The men in both companies wore the same green jacket as the 95th Rifles, with black edged white collar, cuffs and shoulder straps, three rows of pewter buttons, and grey pantaloons.

The **Provincial Marine** was a colonial naval force manning small vessels mostly on lakes Ontario, Erie and Huron. In existence since the second half of the 18th century, its officers had provincial commissions from the Commander-in-Chief and Governor-General of British North America. On 24 June 1813, it was transferred under the authority of a Royal Navy officer, Capt. Richard O'Connor, heading detachments of Royal Navy sailors as reinforcement to serve on the Great Lakes.

Officers of the Provincial Marine wore a uniform very similar to the Royal Navy's, described in the 1790s as 'blue and white, with large yellow buttons with the figure of a beaver, over which is inscribed the word, Canada'. On 3 February 1813, Gen. Sheaffe in Upper Canada was instructed that 'the Uniform of the Officers of His Majesty's [Provincial] Marine on the Lakes to be the same as the Royal Navy, but no Officer at present to rate higher than a Commander' (C1220).

Sailors of the Provincial Marine had slop clothing as in the Royal Navy. Material for the sailors at Amherstburgh in 1813 included material to make blue jackets and trousers with small yellow brass buttons, scarlet waistcoats with small brass buttons, round hats and glazed leather hats. Shirts of blue striped cotton and flannel, red handkerchiefs, strong worsted socks, strong shoes, blue and white thread, tape and twist, Guernsey frocks and pairs of worsted mittens were provided for cold weather. It is obvious from all this that Provincial Marine sailors were clothed in the usual naval style. (For more on Royal Navy dress, see Philip Haythornthwaite's Elite 48 *Nelson's Navy*.)

2 The companies were mistakenly termed 'Canadian Chasseurs' following the Hampton incidents, possibly because they were intended for Canada and were composed of French light infantrymen. See below for the real Canadian Chasseurs.

An officer's coatee, 104th Foot (New Brunswick Regiment), 1812-1817. Scarlet, with light buff collar, cuffs, lapels and turnbacks, it also has silver buttons. (York-Sunbury Museum, Fredericton)

The **Indian Department** was concerned with military and diplomatic relations with the Indian nations of British North America. It was under the authority of a superintendent general who had the military rank of colonel. The establishment was divided between Upper and Lower Canada, each under the command of an assistant-superintendent/lieutenant-colonel with a staff of over 100 captains, lieutenants and interpreters serving with various tribes and in frontier forts. Their diplomatic role was to insure that good relations prevailed between the Indian nations and the British authorities in North America. Their military role was to secure the Indians' alliance in a conflict against the Americans and fight at their side. As a result, individual officers and translators were involved in scores of skirmishes as well as larger engagements during the 1812-1814 war, sometimes leading the Indians.

In the late 18th century, the uniform of the Indian Department was red, apparently with buff facings and silver buttons and lace. At the time of the war of 1812, the department's uniform for its officers was scarlet with green collar, cuffs and lapels, white turnbacks, gold buttons, lace and epaulettes. Naturally, in the wilderness, this would have varied a great deal with many elements of native dress. However, wearing red coats was 'a necessary precaution to prevent being shot by our own Indians', noted Col. Claus.

LOWER CANADA

The Province of Lower Canada – the present-day Quebec – was the most important of the British North American colonies and had the largest reserve of men to draw upon: about 60,000 aged between 16 and 60. The great majority were French Canadians who, as one British officer put it, 'perhaps did not love the English Government or people, but they loved the Americans less'. Thus, the province raised its own regular 'Select Embodied' troops from February 1812, representing an establishment of about 6,500 officers and men. This little army had its reserve, and in an emergency, could be joined within hours by a volunteer militia force. Within a few days, some Sedentary Militia Divisions near the threatened area could be called up. In October 1813, thousands of reserve Sedentary militiamen were called up, some being formed into the 7th and 8th temporary 'Sedentary Embodied Militia' battalions, but all were soon released from service in November. There were some reductions during 1814, but the province kept many permanent service units on a war footing until all were disbanded in March 1815.

The **Canadian Voltigeurs** were raised from April 1812, and also known under their French name of *Voltigeurs canadiens*. It was listed as part of the British regular forces in the Army Returns. They fought in several battles and skirmishes, but it is at Châteauguay, on 26 October 1813, that Lt. Col. Charles-Michel de Salaberry and his Voltigeurs became almost legendary in French Canada. They were disbanded on 24 May 1815.

The 'Conditions' for raising the unit approved on 15 April 1812 called for 'The Clothing to be Grey with black Collar & Cuffs and black Buttons with Canadian Short Boots. Light Bear Skin Caps' (C796). From April 1812, a peaked bearskin cap was issued. Other details are uncertain. In July 1812, de Salaberry reported receiving 134 'pewter bugles' possibly as cap badges, although the bearskin would probably have hidden them. Bearskin caps, to last two years, were issued again in 1813.

Enlisted men wore grey coatees with black collars, cuffs and shoulder straps. They were lined with flannel (probably white), and had black buttons and seven yards of black lace, which was not enough to lace all the buttonholes, so was probably used for edging. There was probably a single row of buttons down the front, and three or four buttons to each cuff and pocket flap. In early January 1813, wings were approved for the uniform, and black lace and fringe was supplied. Meanwhile, Sir George Prevost asked for 'grey cloth' uniforms with 'Black Cuffs and Capes [collar]' for the Voltigeurs to be sent from England (CO 42/148). They arrived in the middle of 1813 and were probably issued in the spring of 1814. These may have been cut in the usual light infantry style and possibly had pointed cuffs and three rows of black buttons in front.

Pantaloons were to be grey, but due to supply difficulties in 1812, poor quality blue ones were instead issued. From 1813, grey pantaloons were issued. Although 'Canadian Short Boots' were mentioned, the Voltigeurs actually always wore shoes. The stocks were of black velvet. White *gilets* – basically a sleeved waistcoat – were also issued.

Buglers appear to have had no particular distinction other than their bugles. Sergeants had nine yards of quality black cotton lace, the extra two yards undoubtedly being for chevrons. The four senior staff sergeants had nine yards of silver lace. Sergeants had sashes, probably the regulation crimson, with a black central line, from 1813. Accoutrements were black, and musket barrels browned.

Officers of the Canadian Voltigeurs wore a distinctive hussar-type uniform consisting of a green dolman with black collar, cuffs, black cords, three rows of black buttons; green pantaloons; a scarlet light infantry sash with cords and tassels; black boots; a fur cap and possibly a green shako with black cord towards the end of the war. Voltigeur officers did not have the black pouch and belt with attached whistle and chain, but simply the silver whistle attached to a narrow black ribbon.

Early in 1812, the legislature of Lower Canada voted £60,000 and authorised Governor-General Sir George Prevost to raise four battalions by embodying militiamen during May and June. A draft of 2,000 bachelors aged from 18 to 30 was to serve up to two years in time of war in the **Lower Canada Select Embodied Militia Battalions**.

Officers were commissioned from 25 May, and by June, the battalions were stationed mostly to the south of Montreal. Following the declaration of war by the United States, the establishment of each battalion was raised to 800 rank and file, and the 5th Battalion was created on 21 September 1812. On 12 March 1814, the 5th was reorganised as light infantry and became the 'Canadian Chasseurs'. The 6th Battalion was authorised on 28 February 1813 to serve as garrison troops in Quebec

Lt. John Le Couteur (1794-1875), wearing the scarlet coatee with light buff collar and lapels, silver buttons and wings of the Light Company, 104th Foot (New Brunswick Regiment), c.1813-1815. Le Couteur saw much action with his regiment and left a remarkable journal, recently published, of his campaigns and of life in Canada. Back in Jersey, his keen intelligence led him into a multitude of endeavours for which he was knighted, made ADC to the Queen and Fellow of the Royal Society. (Société Jersiaise, Jersey)

City, with a smaller establishment of 600 rank and file, reduced in March 1814 to 424 until disbanded on 4 September 1814. The first four battalions remained in service until disbanded on 1 March 1815. Except for the 6th Battalion, all battalions had detachments in action in various engagements during the war.

The first uniforms worn by these battalions are not known in detail. The supplies for the first 2,000 levies included 'red cloth...brown linen for lining ... trousers ... buttons ... hats or caps ... cockades ... private's loopings' and haversacks, as well as fifes and drums and pikes for sergeants (C1218). There is no definite information on the facings adopted by each battalion in 1812. The instructions for the officer's uniforms of the 2nd Battalion called for a red coatee with white collar, cuffs and lapels; narrow gold lace edging the collar and cuffs; a hat according to British regulations; but no epaulettes or sashes for captains or subalterns 'for this year'.

Red cloth became scarce in Canada and, in 1813, green was used for the enlisted men's coatees in some battalions. These green coatees had red collar and cuffs with white lace. Deserters from the 2nd Battalion were described in May and June 1813 as wearing olive-coloured coatees faced red and trimmed with white lace, blue pantaloons and round hats. The 3rd Battalion received, in May 1813, green coatees, blue pantaloons, moccasins, shakos without 'feathers, rosettes and tufts', but with small bugle badges instead of plates (C703). The detachment of the 5th Battalion at Châteauguay in October 1813 was reported in green. However, the 1st Battalion purchased old red coatees of the 103rd Foot, and was even hoping to get surplus coatees from the 8th Foot in March 1813, so probably did not wear green.

During the summer of 1813, a considerable quantity of militia clothing arrived at Quebec from England. On 30 June, the flank companies of the first five battalions and the complete 6th Battalion were ordered an issue of these stores, comprising: 'Caps [shakos] and plumes, Red Coats, Waistcoats with sleeves, Blue Trowsers, Forage Caps, Gaiters, Linen Shirts, Stockings, Shoes, Knapsacks' and 'Stocks and Clasps' (C1221). The facings of each battalion were directed to be as follows: 1st blue; 2nd light green; 3rd yellow; 4th dark green; 5th black; 6th black.[3] As all battalions were short of various accessories, in August, 'boots,

---

3 Some modern sources mention blue, green, light buff and black facings for the first four battalions. This is based on a request for uniforms sent by Sir George Prevost to Earl Bathurst on 21 November 1812, but the actual facings are those given for the battalions in June 1813 and March 1814.

trowsers, gaiters, Caps [shakos] complete and Forage Caps' were ordered to be immediately issued to all companies in all battalions (C1203 1/2 R).

The next and last issue to the battalions appears to have been made in March 1814, consisting of 'Regimental Coats, Trowsers, gaiters & Bucket Caps [shakos]'. Undress jackets (the 'waistcoats with sleeves'), stockings, drawers and other 'necessaries' were also issued later (C1223). The facing colours of some battalions were changed and now stood as follows: 1st blue; 2nd yellow; 3rd green; 4th green.

The 4th Battalion did not receive its clothing immediately, as in September 1814 it complained of not receiving any clothing since June 1813. In any event, most of the battalions were now clothed in red uniforms which, except for the men's shakos, were very similar to those of the British line infantry. It seems that the first five battalions never wore the 'Belgic' shako, as 'bucket' shakos were specified. However, the 6th Battalion may have had the 'Belgic' shako, as their August 1813 issue noted their shakos had 'cords with tufts' (C1220).

It is clear from surviving officer's coatees and portraits that officers of the Select Embodied Militia battalions tried to emulate the dress of their British counterparts. Even if their men wore green at times, all officers always had scarlet coatees. All battalions apparently had gold buttons and lace for their officers. Perhaps the most exceptional feature was the dress of the officers of the Light Company of the 5th Battalion. According to a miniature, this consisted of a scarlet jacket with black collar, no lapels and three rows of small buttons on the breast, a style seen in a few English militia units.

The **Compagnie des Guides** was a cavalry company, also known as the Corps of Guides. It was approved on 25 August 1812 and formed in September. It served in the Montreal area during the war until disbanded on 24 March 1815. They were seen in the middle of September 1812 wearing round hats, grey short jackets and trousers made of corduroy or other material. Each trooper had a waistbelt with a belly cartridge box and was armed with a sabre and a pistol. Their later uniform is unknown.

Lt. William Andrews and 22 gunners, part of the volunteer company of the Montreal Militia, were embodied in September 1812 for full-time service with the **Royal Militia Artillery**. The uniform would have been the same as the Royal Artillery.

The **Corps of Canadian Voyageurs** was a rather unusual corps raised by the North-West Fur Company from among its employees. Formed in October 1812, its objective was to militarise the voyageurs who kept the supplies moving from Montreal to the western outposts. It was disbanded on 14 March 1813, the military supply duties being more properly taken up by the Commissariat which raised the Provincial Commissariat Voyageurs (see below).

Officers of the Canadian Fencibles at Fort Malden in 1813. The officer on the left is dressed in the pre-1812 style, with a bicorn with plume and gold cockade loop and tassels, a long-tailed scarlet coat with yellow collar, cuffs, lapels and white turnbacks, gold epaulette and buttons, white breeches and black boots. The officer on the right, wearing a short-tailed coatee with gold wings, is of the Light Company and is obviously off duty in his white gaiter-trousers and a round hat. Detail from an 1813 water-colour. (Fort Malden National Historic Site, Amherstburgh, Ontario)

This soldier in a boat near Fort Malden in 1813 is seemingly of the Canadian Fencibles. He wears a tall dark blue peaked forage cap with a yellow band, a red fatigue jacket with yellow collar and cuffs. Several other small figures have the same costume with greyish trousers. Detail from an 1813 water-colour. (Fort Malden National Historic Site, Amherstburgh, Ontario)

The officers of the corps had a uniform which remains unknown. The dress of the voyageurs themselves is better known, but again, precise information is lacking. On 1 October 1812, '... at least 500 Voyageurs and their Bourgeois' offered their services to the Governor-General, Sir George Prevost. He proposed to 'dress them in red, but they refused', apparently because the army-style coatees would have been most unsuitable for the voyageur's work. They were inspected by Prevost who intended 'to select 300 of the most robust and well made, to form a battalion; they will wear the capot and the mitasse of red, and will be armed with a pike, a sabre and a pistol', wrote Mrs. Viger.

The voyageurs, who made quite unusual soldiers, were very poor at parade ground tactics, with countless infractions of discipline due to their pranks and cheerfulness. Ross Cox, who reports several hilarious incidents concerning the officers and voyageurs during the War of 1812, wrote that: 'The dress of a voyageur generally consists of a capot made out of a blanket, with leather or cloth trowsers, moccasins, a striped cotton shirt, and a hat or fur cap. They seldom annoy themselves with a waistcoat; and in summer season their necks are generally exposed. They all wear belts of variegated worsted, from which their knives, smoking-bags, &c., are suspended .... When on duty ... [they] generally came on parade with a pipe in their mouth and their rations of pork and bread stuck on their bayonets .... They could not be got to wear stocks; and as such did not use cravats, came on parade with naked necks, and very often with rough beards. In this condition they presented a curious contrast to ... the British soldiery with whom they occasionally did duty.'

All this led many a voyageur to temporary confinement, but it was usually in vain. If the prison guard sentry was a fellow voyageur, he would let out the prisoner telling him to 'go sleep with his woman and come back early the next morning'! But, concluded Cox, Notwithstanding these peculiarities the voyageurs were excellent partisans, and, from their superior knowledge of the country, were able to render material service during the war'.

The **Quebec Volunteers** were raised in Quebec City in mid-November 1812, and were to form an infantry battalion of six companies with a battery of

Brass belt-plate of the 10th Royal Veteran Battalion, 1807-1815. The 10th Royal Veteran Battalion was raised from 1807 for service in Canada. According to Capt. Roberts who commanded the detachment from Fort St Joseph at the capture of Mackinac in 1812, these veteran soldiers were 'so debilitated and worn down by unconquerable drunkenness that neither the fear of punishment, the love of fame or the honour of the country can animate them to extraordinary exertions'. They were also seasoned soldiers when sober, and served with distinction against the Americans in several engagements. The 10th was renumbered as the 4th battalion in June 1815 and disbanded at Quebec on 19 October 1816. (Fort St Joseph National Historic Site, St Joseph Island, Ontario)

1: Queen's Rangers, private, c.1797-1802
2: King's New Brunswick Regiment, private, 1793-1794
3: Royal Canadian Volunteers, private, 1795-1800

A

1: Infantry Officer, 1800-1806
2: Nova Scotia Fencibles, officer, 1804-1812
3: 10th Royal Veterans Battalion, private, 1807-1813

B

1: Canadian Voyageurs, 1812-1815
2: Canadian Voltigeurs, private, 1813
3: Canadian Voltigeurs, officer, 1813

C

1: Upper Canada Militia, private, 1813
2: Royal Newfoundland Fencibles, private, Battalion Company, 1812-1813
3: Upper Canada Militia, officer, 2nd Leeds Rifle Company, c.1812

D

1: Upper Canada Provincial Artificers, private, 1813
2: Upper Canada Militia, private, 1813
3: Canadian Fencibles, drummer, Battalion Company, 1812-1813

E

1: Lower Canada Sedentary Militia, autumn of 1813
2: 3rd Battalion, Lower Canada Select Embodied Militia, private, Light Company, 1813
3: Canadian Light Dragoons, trooper, 1813

F

1: Michigan Fencibles, private, 1814-1815
2: Upper Canada Militia, officer, 1814
3: Glengarry Light Infantry, private, 1812-1816

1: 104th (New Brunswick) Foot, private, Grenadier Company, 1814-1816
2: Indian Department, officer, c. 1813-1815
3: Western (or Caldwell's) Rangers, private, 1813-1815

H

artillery which was never formed. About 50 infantry volunteers mounted guard from 30 December, but the corps was small. It appears that the men, along with some of the officers, were incorporated into the new 6th Battalion of Select Embodied Militia from 13 February 1813. The infantry uniform was red, with purple facings and white lace for the men, the officers having scarlet faced with purple velvet, silver buttons and lace.

The **Corps of Provincial Royal Artillery Drivers** was authorised on 11 January 1813 and formed during April. Attached to the Royal Artillery in the Montreal District, they were disbanded in March 1815. The Artillery Drivers were first allotted a blue jacket with scarlet collar and cuffs, and grey, blue or olive pantaloons with a 'felt cap' (C1220). Uniforms similar to those of the regular Royal Artillery Drivers were later worn. In March 1814, the embodied militiamen serving under the supervision of Capt. Charlton, Royal Artillery Drivers, were issued with helmets with feathers, dress jackets, grey overalls, leather gloves and stocks, boots, spurs and 'Blue guard coats' (C745).

Authorised on 21 January 1813, the **Canadian Light Dragoons** were recruited in the Montreal area during the spring. Its captain was Thomas Coleman and the corps was sometimes known as 'Coleman's Troop'. Sent to Upper Canada where it saw much action, it was disbanded on 24 May 1815.

The uniform was described in a note, apparently by Capt. Coleman, on 2 February 1813, as: 'Blue Jacket, Red Cuff & Collar, White buttons, felt helmet with bear skin – Grey Overalls Wrapped with Leather & Canadian beef Half boots to lace in front' (C703). Nine days later, the uniform is mentioned as: 'Blue Jacket & Grey Overalls, a felt Cap with Bear Skin. The Colour of the Cuffs & Collar may be left to Capt. Coleman's Choice', wrote Governor-General Prevost who was not aware of Coleman's choice. There were also second thoughts on the red facings: on 13 April, Prevost asked that dark blue jackets 'with white Cuffs & Collar & white Buttons' be sent from England for the troop's 1814 issue (C1220).

Embodied on 25 March 1813, the **Dorchester Provincial Light Dragoons** under Capt. William Watson served in Quebec City until disbanded on 24 March 1815. This troop was armed and equipped by the government, but furnished its own horses and was clothed at its own expense. The 1813 uniform is unknown. It received an issue of uniforms in 1814 which may have been blue with white collar and cuffs, the same as Capt. Coleman's Canadian Light Dragoons.

The **Provincial Commissariat Voyageurs** succeeded the Corps of Canadian Voyageurs (see above), and were authorised on 8 April 1813, under the supervision of the Commissariat. The superintendent (or lieutenant-colonel) and deputy-superintendent (major) of this unit were Assistant Commissary-General Clarke and Deputy-Assistant-Commissary-General Finlay who oversaw

Shako badge of the Glengarry Light Infantry, 1813-1816. It probably belonged to an officer as there are traces of silvering. The top part is missing. (Coteau-du-Lac National Historic Site, Coteau-du-Lac, Québec)

Brass belt-plate of the Glengarry Light Infantry, 1812-1816. Although it is inscribed '1st', this regiment had only one battalion. (Niagara Historical Society Museum, Niagara-on-the-Lake, Ontario)

Lt. Thomas Gugy (1798-1825), Glengarry Light Infantry, 1812-1816, wearing a green dolman with black collar, black cords on collar and chest, and silver buttons. Gugy came from a Swiss military family, his father having been an officer in the French army before emigrating to Canada. Young Gugy saw action in the Niagara with his regiment. (Musée du Québec, Quebec City)

the captain, ten lieutenants, ten sergeants (or conductors) and some 400 privates (or voyageurs) from the corps headquarters at Lachine, west of Montreal. This unit was often still called Corps of Canadian Voyageurs right up to its disbandment on 24 March 1815.

The uniform of senior officers was that of the Commissariat. The corps was 'furnished with arms, accoutrements and clothing at the expense of government' (WO 57/14). The enlisted men certainly wore the usual clothing of voyageurs.

By a General Order of 12 April 1813, the flank companies of the first five battalions were ordered grouped into two **Militia Light Infantry Battalions**, but the actual formation appears to have dated only from 30 June. The companies from the battalions continued to be identified as belonging to their own corps and wore their own battalion uniform. At the battle of Châteauguay, they were seén in 'red coats with white cross-belts'. These temporary light infantry battalions were dissolved on 25 November 1813, and the companies went back to their respective battalions.

The **Frontier Light Infantry** was a two-company corps formed in May 1813 to patrol the American border south of Montreal. On 13 August it was attached to the Canadian Voltigeurs and became the ninth and tenth companies of that unit on 10 June 1814, but kept its distinct identity. It was disbanded on 24 March 1815. The uniform was the same as the Canadian Voltigeurs.

The **Independent Company of Militia Volunteers** was formed in May 1813 and attached to the Frontier Light Infantry into which it was amalgamated in February 1814. The unit was to be 'clothed, armed and equipped in the same manner as the Frontier Light Infantry' (RG9, IA3, 5).

Ordered formed on 12 March 1814 by converting the 5th Battalion of the Select Embodied Militia into a light infantry unit of six companies, the **Canadian Chasseurs** were brigaded with the Canadian Voltigeurs and the Frontier Light Infantry. They served in Lower Canada and on the expedition against Plattsburg in September 1814, and were disbanded on 24 March 1815. The uniform was to be similar to that of the Canadian Voltigeurs: grey with black collar, cuffs and shoulder straps, grey wings laced black, possibly three rows of black buttons in front, and grey pantaloons. They probably had the light infantry shako with a green plume. They wore black accoutrements and had browned musket barrels.[4]

LOWER CANADA SEDENTARY MILITIA

The Lower Canada Sedentary Militia, numbering about 54,000 able-bodied men, was organised into a mixture of French and British practices. Among the French-Canadian populace, which provided the vast majority of units, the parish company was still the basic unit, as in the

4 Not be confused with the 'Independent Companies of Foreigners' (see above) which served in a raid on the American coast, and were sometimes erroneously called 'Canadian Chasseurs'.

days of New France, with its captain having a considerable role in the social and civic life of the community. Most villages had one militia company, but some might have more depending on the size of the population. Although considered by Sir George Prevost in 1812 to be 'a mere posse, ill arm'd and without discipline', these rural militiamen were usually very sturdy fellows and often excellent shots. Most were accomplished hunters, and carried their own light-calibre smooth-bore hunting muskets. The parish company of each village belonged to regiment-like 'divisions' of Sedentary Militia, which in turn belonged to one of the province's three districts: Montreal, Trois-Rivières and Quebec. The Eastern Townships had been settled by English-speaking Loyalists and were a separate entity, almost a district of their own. They were organised as an English county militia regiment with six battalions, some battalions having a troop of cavalry.

The vast majority of Lower Canadian Sedentary militiamen had no uniforms. Since the Militia's organisation in the 17th century, the militiamen always wore their own peculiar Canadian civilian dress which was superbly adapted to the country and to the Indian-style skirmishing warfare at which they excelled. Thus, the vast majority of Lower Canadian militiamen in the countryside wore mostly grey homespun capots fastened with a colourful sash. At the beginning of the 19th century, it seems that the wool caps were usually blue in the Montreal area, white in the Trois-Rivières District and red in Quebec. If called on active duty, as many were in the autumn of 1813, they would appear in their civilian dress, be served with British arms and accoutrements which could be black as well as white, and perform some basic drill. Their appearance could be quite impressive as the surgeon of the 89th Foot noted near Montreal:

'We came up with several regiments of militia on their line of march. They had all a serviceable appearance – all had been pretty well drilled, and their arms being direct from the tower, were in perfectly good order, nor had they the mobbish appearance that such a levy in any other country would have had. Their capots and trousers of home-spun stuff, and their blue tuques (night caps) were all of the same cut and color, which gave them an air of uniformity that added much to their military look .... They marched merrily along to the music of their voyageur songs, and as they perceived our uniform as we came up, they set up the Indian War-whoop, followed by a shout of *Vive le Roi* along the whole line...'

In summer, the dress might also consist simply of a grey homespun jacket with a pair of trousers and a

Capt. Jacques Viger, Canadian Voltigeurs, c.1812-1813. This illustration is after a portrait that is now lost. His uniform was described in the 1830s as a green dolman with black facings and cords, and a black fur cap. (Université de Montréal)

Lt. John Hebden, Adjutant of the Canadian Voltigeurs, c.1814-1815. He wears a green shako with black cord and turn-up visor, and green plume; a green dolman with black collar, cuffs, buttons and cords; green pantaloons laced black; a scarlet light infantry sash; a black sabre belt with gilt buckles; a gilt-hilted sabre in black scabbard with gilt fittings; black boots with steel spurs. He holds a bay horse which has black bridles and a green hussar-type pointed schabraque with a green tassel. Print after a portrait. (National Archives of Canada, C25697)

straw hat. Many rural Canadians still wore their hair in a long queue wrapped in an eelskin, and often smoked short pipes.

Officers of rural units, especially junior officers of remote areas, were unlikely to have uniforms. At most, they might have a sword and perhaps a gorget, as in the French regime, to wear with their civilian clothes. Nevertheless, there is evidence that, in the Montreal District in particular, uniforms were worn by many officers, especially field officers of divisions. This appears to have started in the early 1790s, when a blue coat with scarlet collar, cuffs and lapels and long white turnbacks was favoured. A blue coat faced scarlet was still worn by the field officers of the St Ours Militia Division in June 1812, with gold buttons and epaulettes, a round hat with cockade, a white waistcoat, nankeen pantaloons and boots (when changed to a red coat faced green with gold buttons and epaulettes). The Beloeil Division had a scarlet coat with blue collar, cuffs and lapels, the collar having two gold laces on each side (although other buttonholes had no lace), gold buttons, and white turnbacks. A portrait of Major Eustache Desrivières-Beaubien, of the Verchères Division, shows him in a light infantry-style scarlet coatee with a white collar (and presumably cuffs, lapels and turnbacks) edged with gold lace, red wings edged with gold lace and fringes, gilt buttons and gorget. In the Eastern Townships, where the battalions styled themselves 'Royal Eastern Townships Militia', it was probably scarlet faced blue. Round hats were the favoured headgear everywhere. As early as 1803, it was reported that officers of 'many regiments' wore 'small round hats with a plume'.

Militias in Quebec City and Montreal were organised into urban battalions. In Montreal, the 1st Battalion was the city's 'British' militia, gathering the English residents, the 2nd and 3rd Battalions being 'Canadian' militia which meant French Canadian. In Quebec City, the 1st and 2nd Battalions were 'Canadian' and the 3rd was the 'British Militia' battalion. These cities also had companies of militia volunteer cavalry and artillery. The militias in cities were generally better appointed and equipped.

During the 1790s and early 1800s, the Montreal British Militia Battalion wore a blue uniform faced white with gilt buttons. It was changed to scarlet, and sometime before April 1813, the facings became yellow. Until 1812, the French-Canadian 2nd and 3rd Battalions wore blue coats faced red with gold epaulettes and buttons. On 10 November 1812 Governor-General Prevost ordered that this dress be changed as soon as possible to scarlet faced sky blue with gold epaulettes and lace, as their former uniform was similar to that of the American enemy! Officers of the 2nd Battalion found that the sky blue facings became dirty easily, and by order of 10 June 1813, the battalion's facing colour was changed to green, with gold epaulettes and gold lace at the collar and cuffs. There were also two companies of Royal Montreal Artillery

Lt. Col. Charles-Michel de Salaberry (1778-1829), Canadian Voltigeurs, c.1814-1815. The uniform would have been green with black facings, lace and buttons, and a red sash. The gold epaulettes were probably worn when he became Inspecting Field Officer of Light Troops from 11 April 1814. De Salaberry was commissioned in the British Army, along with three of his brothers in the 1790s with the blessings of the Duke of Kent. Two died in India, another at the storming of Badajos. Charles-Michel, who had served in the 60th, raised his light infantry and gained lasting fame in French Canada when the force he was commanding defeated the American army marching on Montreal in October 1813. Engraving after an original portrait, present location unknown. (National Archives of Canada, C9226)

Pierre-René Boucher de la Bruère, 2nd Battalion, Lower Canada Select Embodied Militia, 1813. Bruère was made a captain on 25 May 1812 and a major from 25 March 1813. His scarlet faced white uniform with gold buttons, epaulettes and lace edging the collar and the cuffs (apparently pointed) was worn by the 2nd Battalion in 1812 and 1813. The Musée Pierre-Boucher in Trois-Rivières, Québec, has his 1814-1815 coatee which is scarlet faced yellow with gold buttons and two laces at each side of the collar and has the usual cuffs with buttons, as well as his crimson sash, visible on the portrait. Painting by G. Girouard, dated 1813. (Musée du Québec, Quebec City)

who most likely wore uniforms similar to the Royal Artillery; the uniform of the Royal Montreal Troop of Cavalry was probably blue faced scarlet, with gold buttons and lace in the light dragoon style.

In Quebec City, the 3rd Battalion 'British' Militia adopted in 1803 a uniform of scarlet faced with black velvet, trimmed with gold lace and buttons for officers. The officers of the 1st and 2nd battalions of *Milice canadienne* adopted a blue uniform with red facings and gold epaulettes and buttons. The governor wanted their appearance to be 'similar to ... His Majesty's regular troops', and on 22 July 1805 he ordered the officers and privates to 'be dressed in a red scarlet coat turned up with blue' by September. There were also artillery companies in Quebec City, and they continued to wear blue faced red, probably much the same as the Royal Artillery. A troop of Quebec Light Cavalry was raised in April 1812 and it wore a light dragoon style of uniform: Tarleton helmets, blue cloth forage caps, a black silk handkerchief for a stock, a blue 'dress jacket' with a red collar and silver braid, a plain undress jacket, a white linen stable jacket, brown linen trousers, grey cloth overalls, grey cloth pantaloons, half boots and spurs.

UPPER CANADA MILITIA

The province of Upper Canada was organised as a separate colony following the Constitutional Act of 1791 which split Canada into two colonies. The area west of Montreal had been known as the 'Upper Country' since the French Regime, hence the new colony's name. Broadly, the new colony covered what is now the southern part of the Canadian province of Ontario. It stretched from the present border with Quebec province to the present city of Windsor on Lake Huron, facing Detroit, Michigan. It was divided into eight districts: Eastern, Johnstown, Midland, Newcastle, Home, Niagara, London and Western. Each district had several counties; Essex and Kent counties were in the Western district, for instance.

The Loyalists had provided the first waves of settlers after the American War of Independence but, from the end of the 18th century, many Americans had left the United States to settle in Upper Canada. By 1812, it was estimated that up to half the population was American or of American parents. This was naturally a cause of concern for the British authorities in the event of war with the United States. As it turned out, these fears were unfounded, and the militiamen of Upper Canada served with distinction and perseverance throughout three years of repeated American invasions. Indeed, Upper Canada was the main battlefield of the opposing armies, and suffered considerable devastation as a result, even its capital York (now Toronto) being partly burned by the Americans.

The Militia was organised in 1793 and

Louis J. de Beaujeu, 2nd Battalion, Lower Canada Select Embodied Militia, 1813. He was a captain from 25 May 1812 and major from 17 October 1812. The scarlet faced white uniform with gold buttons, epaulettes and lace was worn by the 2nd Battalion in 1812 and 1813. Painting by G. Girouard, dated 1813. (Musée du Québec, Quebec City)

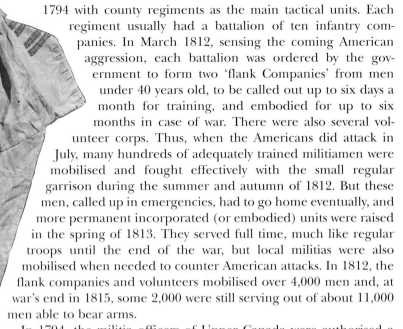

A remarkable relic of the battle of Châteauguay on 26 October 1813. Lt. (later Capt.) François Dezery, Light Company, 3rd Battalion, Lower Canada Select Embodied Militia, was wounded in action on the east bank of the Châteauguay River – probably in the left arm or shoulder – when his company successfully charged a powerful American column in the woods. Blood stains are still on the coat's shoulder area and it is obvious that the left sleeve was torn out at the shoulder seams to treat the wound. The coat itself is the pre-1812 older pattern with long tails. All buttons are missing. It is scarlet with yellow collar, cuffs and lapels, and has white turn-backs and silver lace with a black line. This last detail reveals that, in all likelihood, this is a second-hand officer's coat of the 13th Foot purchased by Dezery, possibly for use in the field. (Canadian War Museum, 79-4799)

1794 with county regiments as the main tactical units. Each regiment usually had a battalion of ten infantry companies. In March 1812, sensing the coming American aggression, each battalion was ordered by the government to form two 'flank Companies' from men under 40 years old, to be called out up to six days a month for training, and embodied for up to six months in case of war. There were also several volunteer corps. Thus, when the Americans did attack in July, many hundreds of adequately trained militiamen were mobilised and fought effectively with the small regular garrison during the summer and autumn of 1812. But these men, called up in emergencies, had to go home eventually, and more permanent incorporated (or embodied) units were raised in the spring of 1813. They served full time, much like regular troops until the end of the war, but local militias were also mobilised when needed to counter American attacks. In 1812, the flank companies and volunteers mobilised over 4,000 men and, at war's end in 1815, some 2,000 were still serving out of about 11,000 men able to bear arms.

In 1794, the militia officers of Upper Canada were authorised a uniform of scarlet faced blue with gilt plain buttons, if they wished to wear one. Surviving artefacts and documents testify that some did. The 1st Lincoln Militia Regiment even bought regimental drums and silver epaulettes for the regimental sergeant major. But most officers and militiamen probably did not undertake the sizeable expense of getting a uniform. In April 1812, militiamen called into the field were advised to provide themselves with 'a short coat of some dark coloured cloth made to button well round the body, and pantaloons suited to the season, with the addition of a round hat'. The officers were to dress like their men 'in order to avoid the bad consequences of a conspicuous dress'. By the end of May, material for clothing was sent to them from Lower Canada to make red coats, possibly faced with yellow, together with 1,000 'felt caps' (shakos), 130 'leather light infantry caps' and over 600 hats (C1218).

Even so, most militiamen in the flank companies were probably not in uniform by the time war was declared. At the siege of Detroit in August, old cast-off uniforms from the 41st Foot (red faced red, white lace with a black line in bastion shape, set evenly) were served out to militiamen which had 'a most happy' effect, 'it having more than doubled our own regular force in the enemy's eyes,' wrote Major-General Sir Isaac Brock.

By the end of the year, red cloth was lacking in Canada and, like in Lower Canada, the militia of Upper Canada was assigned 'green jackets, red cuffs and collar and white lace; blue gunmouth trousers, and a felt regulation cap' by Sir George Prevost on 1 January 1813 (C1220). This was for militiamen called on permanent duty. Many men called out in emergencies had no uniforms at all and wore civilian clothes.

In the spring of 1814, red coats with green facings 'light and dark' with trousers, shoes, shakos, etc., were received for the militia.[5] But blue was the preferred facing colour, and on 21 June 1814, all officers were instructed by General Order to appear 'in a scarlet jacket with dark blue facings, yellow buttons, gold lace round the Collar and Cuffs only, and plain gold epaulettes according to their rank. Grey Pantaloons or Trowsers & Cap according to His Majesty's Regulations for Regiments of the Line, but where such cannot be provided Round Hats will be permitted with a Regulation Feather, Cockade on the left side...' (RG9, IB3, 2). In spite of all these efforts to clothe the militia, supplies were often inadequate. A British officer later recalled of the Upper Canadian militia that 'some had red coats and blue or red facings, some had green coats, but most had no coats at all'.

The **Volunteers of 1812** were company-sized units named after their county. The flank companies provided the infantry, but other volunteer formations provided cavalry and artillery. Nearly all were formed in early 1812, and most were embodied at the beginning of the war in the summer of 1812, some serving into 1813. Although they could be numbered '1st', there was often no second company.

Troops of Cavalry: 1st Leeds, 2nd Grenville, 1st Lennox, 1st Addington, 1st Prince Edward, 1st York, 1st and 2nd Lincoln (Niagara Light Dragoons), 2nd Essex, and 1st Kent.

Artillery Companies: 1st Frontenac, 1st and 2nd Lincoln. Rifle Companies: 1st Grenville, 1st and 2nd Leeds, 1st York, 1st Norfolk, and 1st Oxford.

There was also Capt. Robert Runchey's Coloured Company composed of blacks from Niagara and embodied from 24 October to 24 December 1812, the 1st Essex Marine Company, and a 'car brigade' of artillery drivers.

Little is known of the uniforms, if any, worn by these units. Generally, the officers and perhaps some of the men would have had the province's scarlet faced blue uniform. However, a green coat faced black trimmed with gold lace is known to have belonged to an officer of the 2nd Leeds Rifle Company. Some men of Runchey's Coloured Company may have had green coats as the Glengarry Light Infantry.

There were a number of companies of **Provincial Light Dragoons**. The Niagara Provincial Light Dragoons, a troop of 50 'fine young men, but badly mounted and equipped in every way', was raised from 3 March 1813 under Capt. William Merritt, and served in the Niagara frontier area. Renamed the 'Niagara Frontier Guides' on 24 October 1814 and reduced to 25 officers and men, it was disbanded on 24 March 1815. The

Capt. Jean-Baptiste Larue, Grenadier Company, 4th Battalion, Lower Canada Select Embodied Militia, 1813-1815. He wears a scarlet coatee with green collar, plain gold buttons and lace (note the stitching on both sides), gold wings on scarlet with silver flaming grenade, a gold gorget engraved with 'GR' and a crown held with green ribbons, a white belt with gilt oval belt-plate engraved with 'GR' and crown.
(Private collection)

5 A document of 21 May 1814 announcing clothing for 1,000 privates and 40 sergeants states 'The Coats to be green and Yellow Facing an equal number of each' (C1223). This has sometimes been interpreted as a green coat faced yellow, but the last part of the phrase may well indicate that these were red coats, half of the shipment being faced with green, the other half faced yellow. Indeed, this might even be the same shipment of coats reported in the spring of 1814 with green 'light and dark' facings. In any event, blue was confirmed as the facing colour in June.

Officer's gorget and belt-plate of the 6th Battalion, Lower Canada Select Embodied Militia, 1813-1814. The 6th, whose officers were prosperous citizens from Quebec City, was one of the few militia units with its own insignia. The gorget is gilded with custom engravings and the belt-plate was of gilt with crown, letters and scroll in silver.
(Private collection)

Officer's coat of the 1st Battalion, Montreal British Militia, 1790s. Blue with white collar, cuffs, lapels and turnbacks, gilt buttons. (Canadian War Museum, Ottawa)

uniform was to be as the Canadian Light Dragoons of Lower Canada (see Coleman's Troop above) but, although blue jackets are noted, the Upper Canada troop was reportedly poorly equipped.

Two other Provincial Light Dragoon troops, Capt. Andrew Adams' and Capt. Richard Fraser's, were raised during April 1813 in eastern Upper Canada, Adams' troop being amalgamated into Fraser's troop on 25 September 1813. Used mostly for carrying dispatches and patrols, they were issued with artillery jackets, pantaloons, round hats and greatcoats, and were disbanded 24 February 1814.

The **Incorporated Artillery Company** was raised in March 1813, and served at York (Toronto) and in the Niagara. It was also called the Provincial or Militia Artillery, and consisted of artillerymen and drivers. In April 1813, the Militia Artillery coats and Militia Gunner Drivers' jackets were described of 'blue Cloth with Scarlet Collar & Cuffs. The Pantaloons or Trowsers to be of Grey, blue, or olive Cloth', the gunners having trousers and the drivers with pantaloons. All had 'Felt caps' which were probably stovepipe shakos (C1220). Uniforms similar to the Royal Artillery were sent from England to Upper Canada and probably worn from April 1814 until the unit was disbanded on 24 March 1815.

The **Provincial Royal Artillery Drivers** were formed on 3 March 1813 to assist the regular Royal Artillery in moving the guns. Having served in the Niagara peninsula, it was disbanded on 24 March 1815. The first uniform was a 'Jacket 'of blue Cloth with Scarlet Collar & Cuffs & the Pantaloons, Grey, Blue, or Olive, with felt Caps' (C1220). Uniforms similar to the Royal Artillery Drivers were sent from England for the company and probably worn from April 1814.

Authorised on 3 March 1813, the **Corps of Provincial Artificers** was formed to assist the Royal Engineers to which it was attached. It was also known as the 'Coloured Corps' as the enlisted men were all blacks, and most were veterans of Capt. Runchey's Coloured Company. They served in the Niagara peninsula, and were disbanded on 24 March 1815. The first uniform was a blue jacket 'with black Collar & Cuffs' with grey pantaloons and round hats (C1220). Later, uniforms similar to those of the regular Royal Sappers and Miners were sent from England for the company, and probably worn from April 1814.

The **Incorporated Militia Battalion** was authorised formed from 18 March 1813 with 'strong and healthy' militiamen embodied for permanent service. Also called the 'Volunteer Incorporated Militia' battalion, various companies were embodied at Prescott, Kingston, York (Toronto) and the Niagara during the spring of 1813. The 13 companies were united, reorganised and trained as a ten-company battalion at York in March 1814, and sent to the Niagara in July where it saw much action. It was disbanded on 24 March 1815.

The first uniform of the battalion, issued in the spring of 1813, was probably the green jacket with red collar and cuffs, white lace, blue trousers and stovepipe shako. In June 1813, it was sent red coats with green facings, grey trousers, gaiters, shoes, shakos, and forage caps, but these may have been actually issued only in the spring of 1814. In June 1814, it was specified that blue was now to be used for the facings.

Also called Caldwell's Rangers, the **Western Rangers** were formed in April 1813 with volunteers from western Upper Canada to serve with Indians under the command of William Caldwell Sr., a Loyalist noted for

ABOVE **Col. René-Amable Boucher, Seigneur de Boucherville (1735-1812), Boucherville Militia, c.1793,** wearing a blue coat with a red collar, cuffs and lapels, silver buttons and narrow buttonhole lace, and a white waistcoat. Col. de Boucherville was from one of the most distinguished and influential families of the Old Regime gentry in French Canada, and had fought against the Americans in 1775. (Musée de Vaudreuil, Vaudreuil, Canada)

ABOVE, MIDDLE **Capt. François Corbin, Sorel Militia, 1797.** He wears a blue coat with red collar and lapels, silver buttons and epaulette, and a white waistcoat. Sorel is a town about 80 km east of Montreal. Signed and dated pastel 'Louis Dulongpré, Sorel, avril 1797'. (Château de Ramezay Museum, Montreal)

ABOVE, RIGHT **Lt. Col. Pierre Guy, 2nd Battalion, Montréal City Militia, c.1810-1812,** wearing a blue coat with scarlet collar, cuffs and lapels, gold buttons and epaulettes, and gilt-hilted pattern 1803 infantry officer's sabre. Copy after an original portrait now lost. (Château de Ramezay Museum, Montreal)

his anti-American actions as far back as the 1790s. He was succeeded by William Elliott on 24 May 1814. The corps had two companies and was in action in several important engagements, before being disbanded on 24 March 1815. The uniform was suited to its bush-fighting role, and consisted of a 'dark green jacket, grey pantaloons, and a low bucket cap, quite plain' (C797).

The **Loyal Kent Volunteers** were a company of volunteer militiamen in Kent County formed on 25 November 1813. Attached to the Incorporated Battalion on 25 February 1815, they were disbanded on 24 March 1815.

Although not formally authorised, the **Loyal London Volunteers** were nevertheless embodied in the small town of London, Upper Canada, from 24 November 1813, and disbanded on 24 February 1814.

The **Loyal Essex Volunteers** were embodied from about March 1814. Sometimes called 'The Essex Rangers', they served in the London area and the Niagara, before being disbanded on 24 March 1815.

THE INDIAN COUNTRY

The Indian Country, also called the Western Country, denoted the vast unsettled areas to the west where the fur trade was conducted. This broadly included the western Great Lakes and the upper Mississippi valley. A few American and British forts were scattered in this region, and served as bases for fur traders and voyageurs who were largely French Canadians. The British and Canadians in Fort St Joseph (Ontario) took the initiative, captured Fort Mackinac (Michigan) which became their main base and eventually expelled the Americans from northern Michigan and Wisconsin.

The **Michigan Fencibles** was a company of about 45 officers and men raised at Fort Mackinac from September 1813 from voyageurs and fur traders for permanent service. They were part of the garrison of Fort Mackinac, and a small detachment was at Fort Shelby (Wisconsin). They were disbanded at Mackinac on 28 June 1815. In the autumn of 1813, the unit was sent 42 suits of clothing which included 'Red jackets with Black facings ... from the supply recently received from England' (C1221).

For the expedition which led to the capture of the American Fort Shelby at Prairie du Chien (Wisconsin) in July 1814, several units of mostly French Canadian volunteers were formed. The **Mississippi Volunteers** initially had about 65 men in June 1814, but this grew considerably as they made their way towards Prairie du Chien. Lt. James Keating, a former Royal Artillery sergeant, led the 'Mississippi Volunteer Artillery'. A volunteer detachment of Green Bay (Wisconsin) Militia was also present. Thomas Anderson of the Mississippi Volunteers later wryly

Quebec City Militia, 3rd Battalion 'British Militia' colour, 1805. There is a black field with a red cross; the Union Flag was made larger covering the complete upper quarter, as was the cross; a central shield with the gold letters 'QUEBEC MILITIA 1775' is surrounded by a rose and thistle wreath in a natural colour. The King's colour had similar ornaments. It was presented at Quebec on 4 June 1805 by Lady Milne to Colonel Hale. In his reply to Lady Milne, Colonel Hale mentioned that the 'year 1775 is engraved upon most of the ornaments of our uniform: We now see it upon our Colours...'. (Canadian War Museum, Ottawa)

Private's coatee of the Grenadier Company, probably worn by the 3rd Battalion Quebec City 'British' Militia, c.1803 to c.1815. It is red with black collar, cuffs and shoulder straps, white lace set in pair, red wings trimmed with white lace and fringes on the top, which also have a red grenade on a black outline. Note the double loops on the collar instead of the usual 'all around' lacing. The buttons are not original. (Canadian War Museum, Ottawa)

recalled his time as 'a Captain of pompous dimensions', wearing 'a red coat, mustered a couple of epaulettes and an old rusty sword, with a red cock feather adorning my round hat'. The men of these units, however, wore their own typical French Canadian voyageur costume.

MILITIAS OF THE ATLANTIC COLONIES

The **Nova Scotia Militia** numbered about 12,000 men divided into 26 battalions spread across the colony's 12 counties. Each county had several battalions which were known by the county name. During the French naval scare in 1793, Halifax had a fully armed infantry battalion and an artillery company, while a 'Legion of Militia' consisting of infantry with a company of artillery and a company of cavalry was organised to help defend the Annapolis Valley on the Bay of Fundy. Later, some battalions had artillery companies attached, and from 1813, each battalion was authorised to form a light infantry and a rifle company. During the war of 1812-15, about 500 men were embodied and divided into small detachments. They did coastguard duty and had the occasional scuffles with privateers. Another 400 were detailed to escort and guard prisoners-of-war.

The volunteer artillery in the city of Halifax had uniforms which were similar to the Royal Artillery. In 1809 the artillery company of the township of Liverpool, the 21st Battalion, wore 'Blue Round Jackets with red cuff and cape [collar] ... Blue Trowsers, Black Cockades and Feathers, their Equipment perfectly Uniform and Complete'. While many officers and some specialised companies were in uniform at the outbreak of the war, the vast majority of ordinary militiamen wore civilian clothes. The governor therefore asked that uniforms, arms, accoutrements and equipment be sent from Britain. The clothing was sent in August 1813, some of it new and some used. It included 'dark blue facing cloth' and 'White Looping' (CO 42/155).

The **New Brunswick Militia** numbered about 4,500 men, and in December 1812, about 500 men drafted from their local battalions were called out to active duty to replace the 104th Foot about to depart for central Canada. The militiamen at Fredericton and St John were relieved

from duty in March with the arrival of a detachment of the 8th Foot. However, the company at St Andrews remained embodied, and at Fort Cumberland, a small militia force relieved a departing detachment of the 104th Foot. The militia's main preoccupation was countering coastal raids by small American vessels.

Unit commanders decided the type of uniform worn. The St John Volunteer Artillery Company, for example, wore the same as the Royal Artillery. But many officers had no uniforms or had to improvise: one colonel had 'a moveable red cape [collar] upon his Sabbath day blue [civilian coat], and some silk around his waist' [an officer's crimson silk sash]. In late April 1813, uniforms for over 3,000 militiamen were shipped out of England. It appears that the coatees were the standard red infantry style ornamented with white lace, 2,000 with white facings, and 1,000 with blue facings at the collar, cuffs and shoulder straps. Accoutrements were black. Each militiaman was also to have a waistcoat, a pair of trousers, a forage cap, a greatcoat, a stock and clasp, a pair of shoes, a haversack, a canteen, a shako with a shako cover and a shako plate. By the time this shipment arrived in St John, the militia had nearly all gone home except the Charlotte County Militia company at St Andrews.

There was no organised **Newfoundland Militia** outside the port city of St John's. From May 1793 to 1795, there was a four-company corps of volunteers clothed in an unknown uniform. In April 1804, a 200-strong Volunteer Armed Association was formed, and in October 1806, a uniformed five-company unit, the 'Loyal Volunteers of St John's', was in existence. From 12 August 1812, the unit was called St John's Volunteer Rangers. Each private had to purchase 'a cap, jacket, pantaloons and gaiters'. The uniform is not specified, but it appears to have been the green jacket like the rifle battalions of the 60th. The accoutrements, however, were white. The American menace soon subsided and the St John's Volunteer Rangers were disbanded during June and July of 1814.

The **Island of St John/Prince Edward Island Militia** was formed from three militia regiments: Queen's County, King's County and Prince County. Charlottetown, the capital, had several volunteer companies. The volunteers wore uniforms, and although militia regimental officers were ordered to be in uniform by 1 September 1814, the details remain unknown. However, the remnants of a coatee which may have belonged to an officer of the 3rd Battalion, Queen's County Regiment, indicate that it was blue faced red, had white turnbacks with red hearts and gold buttons; this may have been the 1814 uniform.

Cape Breton, a large island, now part of Nova Scotia, was then a separate colony with its own governor at the time of the Napoleonic wars. There were an estimated 1,300 men able to bear arms spread along the island's coast. In 1813, the **Cape Breton Island Militia** was divided into 20 divisions which were like companies as each was commanded by a captain and two lieutenants. There appears to have been a uniform of sorts. At the first muster of the Cape Breton Militia at Sydney, in August 1813, the 'regular uniform for the officers was a blue jacket, gold esplanate [epaulets], black waist belts, sabre, grey overalls and a round hat with feather. The rank and file wore costumes of every imaginable description...'

Bermuda was under the authority of the governor-general of British North America at the time of the Napoleonic wars. It served as an important base for British raids on the American coast during the war with the United States. The **Bermuda Militia** consisted of an infantry company for each of the nine parishes of the colony, with a Troop of Horse grouped into a 'Bermuda Regiment of Militia'. The cavalrymen were all to be uniformed, probably in blue faced red with gilt buttons. All infantrymen were to have muskets, bayonets, cross belts and a cartridge box holding at least 18 rounds. All infantry officers and privates were also to be in uniform, and each parish company chose its own. For instance, on 25 July 1812, the Devonshire Company required its

Officer's coat, 3rd Battalion Quebec City 'British' Militia, c.1803-1813. It is scarlet with black velvet collar, cuffs and lapels, white turnbacks, gold buttons, lace and epaulettes. This unit was one of the very few Canadian militia corps to have a distinctive button, most likely worn from 1803. The date 1775, also on their colours, was in commemoration of the militia's contribution to the successful defence of the city against the Americans in 1775-1776. (Canadian War Museum, Ottawa)

Maj. (later Lt. Col.) Des Rivières-Beaubien, Verchères Division, Lower Canada Sedentary Militia, 1813, wearing a scarlet coat with white collar, edged with gold lace, gilt buttons and gorget, scarlet wing with gold lace and fringes. This division was formed in February 1813 and was embodied from September to November of 1813. Painting by G. Girouard. (Musée du Québec, Quebec City)

members to have: '...a Scarlet Coat with a black cape [collar], Cuff, and Skirt edged with white, to be single breasted, and button up to the throat with Yellow Metal Buttons, a Black Hat with a white feather to be ... above the crown, a black cravat, white waistcoat and trowsers with black gaiters underneath. The dress of the Officers to be the same as privates with the distinction of an epaulette, Sword, Sash....' The uniforms of other companies are unknown.

SELECT BIBLIOGRAPHY

Manuscripts: The great majority of sources used for this study are from archival documents, regrettably impossible to footnote in this short monograph. Most were found at the National Archives of Canada: RG 8 (especially C series), RG 9, MG 23 and MG 24. Many are also at the Public Records Office: Colonial Office 42 (Canada), 188 (New Brunswick), 194 (Newfoundland), 217 (Nova Scotia), 226 (Prince Edward Island); Treasury 1 and 64; War Office 1 (In-letters), 3 (Commander in Chief, Out-letters), 17 (Returns), 27 (Inspections), 57 and 58 (Commissariat).
Public Archives of Nova Scotia, Military Records.
Archives of Bermuda: Acts, Military and Militia Records.
Canadian War Museum: J.N. & B. Pearse notebook.
Anne S.K. Brown Military Collection, Brown University, Providence, USA: Sumner notebooks, Todd Albums.

BOOKS AND ARTICLES

Chambers, Ernest, *The Canadian Marine*, Ottawa, 1905.
Chambers, Ernest, *History of the Canadian Militia*, Ottawa, 1907.
Chartrand, René, *Canadian Military Heritage*, Vol. 2, 1755-1871, Montreal, 1995.
Cruikshank, Ernest A., 'Records of Services of Canadian Regiments during the War of 1812', *Selected Papers of the Royal Canadian Military Institute, 1893-1916.*
Dunnigan, Brian L., *The British Army at Mackinac 1812-1815*, Mackinac, 1980.
Facey-Crowther, David, *The New Brunswick Militia 1787-1867*, Fredericton, 1990.
Jackson, H.M., *The Queen's Rangers in Upper Canada*, Toronto, c.1960.
Graves, Donald E., ed., *Merry Hearts Make Light Days: the War of 1812 Journal of Lieutenant John Le Couteur*, 104th Foot, Ottawa, 1993.
Gray, William, *Soldiers of the King: The Upper Canadian Militia 1812-1815*, Erin (Ontario), 1995.
Irving, L. Homfray, *Officers of the British*

This Upper Canada Militia officer's coat, c.1800-1813, is scarlet with blue collar, cuffs (and lapels which are buttoned across), white turnbacks, white piping edging the bottom of the collar, the lapels, the pocket flaps and the top of the cuffs, gilt buttons, and has one slip of gold lace on each side of the collar. (Fort Malden National Historic Site, Amherstburgh, Ontario)

The coat of Col. Matthew Elliott, 1st Regiment, Essex Militia, Upper Canada, c.1800-1813. It is scarlet with blue collar, cuffs and lapels edged with white piping, white turnback, plain flat gilt buttons. There is a button on each side of the collar. The epaulettes are missing. Matthew Elliott (c.1739-1814), trader, former officer of the British Indian Department, and Member of Upper Canada Legislative Assembly, was a leading figure in the Canadian Northwest border area. He was with his militiamen at the capture of Detroit, at the battle of Frenchtown (or the 'Raisin' – 22 January 1813) and at Miami in May. (Fort Malden National Historic Site, Amherstburgh, Ontario)

Forces in Canada during the War of 1812, Toronto, 1908.

Lépine, Luc, *Lower Canada's Militia Officers 1812-1815; Les officiers de milice du Bas-Canada 1812-1815*, Montreal, 1996.

Nicholson, G.W.L., *The Fighting Newfoundlander*, Government of Newfoundland, 1964.

Mackay, Daniel S.C., 'The Royal Canadian Volunteers', *Organisation of Military Museums of Canada Journal*, 1977.

Piers, Harry, 'Regiments raised in Nova Scotia', *Collections of the Nova Scotia Historical Society*, 1927.

Smith, Charles Hamilton, *Costume of the Army of the British Empire*, London, 1815.

Squires, W. Austin, *The 104th Regiment of Foot (The New Brunswick Regiment) 1803-1817*, Fredericton, 1962.

Sutherland, Stuart, 'Independent Companies of Foreigners: Britain's French Bandits', *Military Illustrated*, December 1996.

Webber, David, *A Thousand Young Men: The Colonial Volunteer Militia of Prince Edward Island 1775-1874*, Charlottetown, 1990.

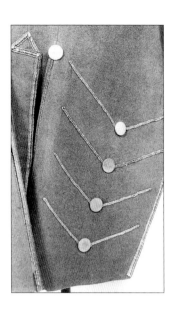

ABOVE **Coatee of Lt. Levi Soper, Rifle Company, 2nd Leeds Militia Regiment, Upper Canada, 1812-1815. Green with black collar, cuffs and lapels, silver buttons, lace and twist cord at the buttonholes. (Old Fort York, Toronto)**

ABOVE RIGHT **Detail of the skirt of Lt. Soper's coatee. (Old Fort York, Toronto)**

THE PLATES

A1: Queen's Rangers, private, c.1797-1802 The early dress of this unit was to be green faced blue, but the facing colour was soon changed to black. Our figure is based on a small coloured sketch by Charles Hamilton Smith, showing the green jacket trimmed with white buttonholes, and the early shako with the bugle horn badge worn by several corps at the time. The Queen's Rangers' outstanding contribution to the settlement of early Ontario is still celebrated today, and its traditions are carried on by a Canadian Militia regiment bearing the same name. (Houghton Library, Harvard University)

A2: King's New Brunswick Regiment, private, 1793-1794 The dress of this unit demonstrates the difficulties that many new units raised in the Atlantic colonies had in obtaining uniforms. According to a surviving bayonet belt with the regimental belt-plate, the accoutrements were black. (Canadian War Museum, Ottawa)

A3: Royal Canadian Volunteers, private, 1795-1800 The dress of this unit was rather original in several ways. It did not make some of the changes in the dress of infantry units. The hats continued to have white edging, red waistcoats were worn after 1797 instead of white, and its coats appear to have had lapels right up to 1802. All these were made from material sent from England to Lower Canada where the uniforms were then assembled. This was an unusual practice as, generally, uniforms were sent out ready-made. Stovepipe shakos were adopted from 1800-01.

B1: Infantry Officer, 1800-1806 This British infantry officer is dressed for duty in Canada during the late autumn or early spring, according to the General Orders of July 1800. The furcrested round hat was in use until 1806, and the blue greatcoat changed to grey in late 1811.

B2: Nova Scotia Fencibles, officer, 1804-1812 Officers of the Nova Scotia Fencibles all wore shakos, by permission, from 1804. Their dress was otherwise similar to other regular and fencible regiments in British North America. (Miniature of Lt. Schwartz; WO 3/336)

B3: 10th Royal Veterans Battalion, private, 1807-1813 The 10th, like all Royal Veteran Battalions, wore red faced blue, the enlisted men's lace being white with a blue line, square-ended and set in pairs. The officers had gold buttons and lace. The breeches and stovepipe shako may have been worn into 1813. The detachment at Mackinac lacked greatcoats in 1812 and wore locally made voyageur-style blanket coats instead. (W.H. Wood, ed., *Select Documents on the Canadian War of 1812*, Toronto, 1920, Vol. I)

C1: Canadian Voyageurs, 1812-1815 A typical voyageur might be a young farmer's son hired to be part of a canoe crew to transport trade goods to the West. He soon became a hardened and thorough canoe man, a strong carrier of heavy bales, and occasional small trader and hunter. Voyageurs had their own utilitarian costume which was generally as shown in this plate. In the warm and humid Canadian summer, however, they might only wear a shirt, breechclouts and moccasins. (G. Dugas, *Un Voyageur des pays d'en haut, Montreal, 1924*; Grace Lee Nute, *The Voyageur*, New York, 1931)

C2: Canadian Voltigeurs, private, 1813 This light infantry unit was to be armed with 'carbines' and black accoutrements in 1812, the carbines apparently being simply India Pattern muskets with bayonets. The voltigeurs were a cheerful group, and used to say that their cartridge boxes were full of 'pills for Yankees'. (C386, C1218; Jacques Viger, 'Ma Saberdache' Mss, Vol. 2, Archives du Séminaire de Québec)

C3: Canadian Voltigeurs, officer, 1813 The officers in this unit wore a hussar-style dark green uniform trimmed with black. The fur cap seems to have been worn from 1812, although Hebden's portrait, reproduced in this book, shows a strange dark green shako. A list of belongings of an officer also mentions a surtout, certainly for undress, and probably single-breasted with long skirts, dark green with black collar, cuffs and buttons, but no cords.

D1: Upper Canada Militia, private, 1813 Many a militiaman came out fighting in civilian dress, as at the battle of Fort George in May 1813, The Reverend John Carrol recalled 'the militia men pouring into the house to receive a badge of white cotton or linen on the arm to let the Indians know we were British'. White seems to have been a popular badge, for it was used again by Upper Canada militiamen in 1837-8. (*Reminiscences of Niagara*, Welland, Ontario, c.1902)

D2: Royal Newfoundland Fencibles, private, Battalion Company, 1812-1813 During 1812 and into 1813, most regular units on campaign wore grey trousers and stovepipe shakos. Besides its white breeches, the Royal Newfoundland Fencibles had trousers which may have been grey or blue in 1812. The men also had white undress jackets with blue collar and cuffs. The regiment saw much action, detachments being deployed as far west as Ohio and Mackinac. (NAC, RG9, IA1, 2; *Montreal Gazette*, 23 March 1812)

D3: Upper Canada Militia, officer, 2nd Leeds Rifle Company, c.1812 From 25 May 1812, rifle companies were authorised, to be recruited from volunteers. No uniform was specified, but the coatee of Lt. Levi Soper of the Rifle Company of the 2nd Leeds Regiment was green faced black with gold buttons and lace. The cut is surprisingly close to the dress worn by some American rifle units. Other details are unknown, but round hats and green pantaloons would be most likely. (Old Fort York, Toronto)

Titus Greer Simons, c.1814-1815. He was commissioned major in the 2nd Regiment of York Militia in 1811 and was later a major in the Upper Canada Volunteer Incorporated Battalion on 25 March 1813. He was wounded at Lundy's Lane on 25 July 1814. He wears a scarlet coatee, with dark blue piped white collar and lapels, gold buttons, epaulettes and lace around the collar, a crimson sash, and a black sword waist-belt with brass snake clasps. (Print after portrait)

E1: Upper Canada Provincial Artificers, private, 1813 This unit was probably the first in Canada to embody blacks for regular service. It served mostly in Burlington and Fort George until disbanded in 1815. Its first uniform of blue faced black was apparently based on the undress of the Royal Military Artificers.

E2: Upper Canada Militia, private, 1813 Due to cloth shortages, green coatees and blue trousers were issued in early 1813 to mobilised militiamen. Pewter bugles were used instead of brass plates on shakos.

E3: Canadian Fencibles, drummer, Battalion Company, 1812-1813 Thanks to a tailor's notebook, the drummer's coat was known to have ten square-ended laced buttonholes set in pairs, 27 yards of narrow lace, and sleeves with six dart chevrons pointing up. The complicated lace pattern is according to an original piece glued on the notebook's page. The drum was painted yellow and the insignia in front was probably about the same as on the colours. (Pearse Notebook and regimental colours, Canadian War Museum)

F1: Lower Canada Sedentary Militia, autumn of 1813 This figure reconstructs the general appearance of rural French Canadian sedentary militiamen who were called out in an emergency. The costume is the typical dress, largely home-made and homespun, worn in the countryside consisting of a capot (usually grey) with a multi-coloured sash around the waist, breeches, long boot-like moccasins and a wool cap. When mustered, the men were issued arms, ammunition and accoutrements which could be white or black. (John Lambert, *Travels...*, London, 1814)

F2: 3rd Battalion Lower Canada Select Embodied Militia, private, Light Company, 1813 The flank companies of the battalions were clothed with new uniforms in the summer of 1813. In the autumn, the Light Company of the 3rd Battalion was with Lt. Col. De Salaberry's advance force when it met with General Wade Hampton's American army moving up towards Montreal along the Châteauguay River. During the battle of 26 October, Hampton sent a strong column in the wood on the east side of the river to outflank the Canadian position, but it ran into Capt. Daly's 3rd Light Company and a company of Sedentary Militia. Daly ordered his men to charge, destabilising the much stronger American column which turned and fled. (*Military Illustrated*, December 1986-January 1987)

F3: Canadian Light Dragoons, trooper, 1813 Capt. Coleman chose the practical uniform shown here for his troop which was soon deployed in Upper Canada and fought in several engagements. This dress was probably worn from the spring of 1813 to early 1814.

G1: Michigan Fencibles, private, 1814-1815 This small unit was recruited from fur traders and voyageurs in Mackinac to reinforce the small regular garrison. It was sent red coatees faced with black, and may have had blue or grey trousers. The 'Belgic' shako is shown, but hats may also have been 'stovepipes'. It is likely that moccasins would have been commonly worn by the men of this unit.

G2: Upper Canada Militia, officer, 1814 After much upheaval due to lack of material and the American invasions, the situation had stabilised enough by 1814 to remind officers that they should be wearing scarlet faced with blue, with gold buttons and lace edging the cuffs and collar, and grey pantaloons. Shakos would have been worn by Incorporated Militia officers, but for many others, round hats were the standard.

G3: Glengarry Light Infantry, private, 1812-1816 This 'Scottish' unit was dressed in green faced black, like the 95th Rifles. They were not armed with rifles, however, but with muskets and had black accoutrements. It had a short but intense service life, seeing much action and earning praise for its distinguished service. The memory of this excellent regiment is still alive in eastern Ontario, and its traditions are carried on. (Ian Kemp, 'Glengarry Light Infantry', *Military Illustrated*, December 1994; W. Boss, *The Stormont, Dundas and Glengarry Highanders*, Ottawa, 1952 & 1996).

H1: 104th (New Brunswick) Foot, private, Grenadier Company, 1814-1816 The coatee worn by this figure is based an a surviving garment captured by an American privateer in late 1812. The facings are shown as white on the coatee, but 'buff' facings were sometimes actually white. On the other hand, the officers of the 104th certainly had light buff facings, as were the regimental colours. The wings on the coatee have no tufts or fringes. From the early 1800s, grenadiers serving overseas were issued shakos instead of bearskin caps. The regiment's 'Belgic' shako plates had '104' below the cipher. (Cape Ann Historical Society Museum, Cape Ann, Massachusetts)

H2: Indian Department, officer, c. 1813-1815 This figure is based on a portrait of William McKay, an officer of the Indian Department who served at Mackinac. It shows a richly laced coatee, probably worn with a bicorn or, on less formal occasions, a round hat. McKay was also a detached captain in the 5th Bn. Lower Canada Select Embodied Militia, and was appointed to command the Michigan Fencibles at Mackinac in 1814. For the portrait, made about 1816 for a fellow officer departing for Scotland, it was specified that McKay be shown in the Indian Department's uniform. In 1823, it was changed to an all green uniform with round hats. (McCord Museum of Canadian History, Montreal)

H3: Western (or Caldwell's) Rangers, private, 1813-1815 This light infantry unit was to serve with allied Indians and had close ties with the Indian Department. It was led by Capt. William Caldwell until he was replaced by James Askin in May 1814. It had a most practical uniform consisting of a plain green jacket without any facings, and a 'low bucket cap' which was apparently a cut-down stovepipe shako with the plate removed.

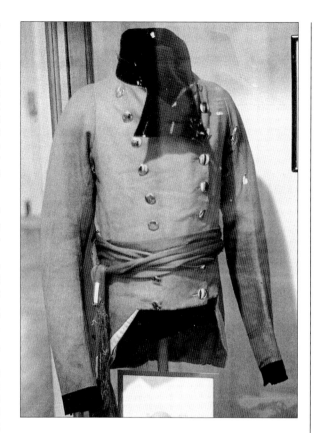

ABOVE **Upper Canada Militia officer's coatee, c.1813-1820. This very plain and obviously locally made garment is scarlet with a very dark blue collar, lapels and small cuffs. There are gilt buttons at each side of the collar and in two rows down the front, but not on the cuffs. The epaulette is missing and the buttons on the chest are modern replacements. The crimson sash was worn around the waist. (Niagara Historical Society Museum, Niagara-on-the-Lake, Ontario)**

BELOW **Brass belt-plate, Nova Scotia Volunteer Artillery, c.1804-1815. (The Army Museum, Halifax Citadel)**

Notes sur les Planches en Couleur

A1 Queen's Rangers, simple soldat, v. 1797-1802. Il porte la veste verte ornée de boutonnières blanches et le premier modèle de shako avec le badge en forme de clairon que portaient plusieurs corps à l'époque. **A2** King's New Brunswick Regiment, simple soldat, 1793-1794. La tenue vestimentaire de cette unité démontre les difficultés que rencontraient un grand nombre de nouvelles unités levées dans les colonies atlantiques pour obtenir des uniformes. **A3** Royal Canadian Volunteers, simple soldat, 1795-1800. Cette unité n'apporta pas les modifications faites à la tenue des unités d'infanterie. Les shakos sont toujours bordés de blanc, les gilets rouges étaient utilisés après 1797 au lieu des gilets blancs et il semble que les vestes à courtes basques comportaient des revers jusqu'en 1802.

B1 Officier d'infanterie, 1800-1806 en uniforme vers la fin de l'automne ou le début du printemps. Le shako rond avec cimier en fourrure fut utilisé jusqu'en 1806 et la veste bleue à courtes basques devint grise à la fin de 1811. **B2** Nova Scotia Fencibles, officier, 1804-1812. Les officiers des Nova Scotia Fencibles portèrent tous un shako, par autorisation, à partir de 1804. A part cela, leur uniforme était semblable à celui des autres régiments réguliers et de milice en Amérique du Nord Britannique. **B3** 10th Royal Veterans Battalion, simple soldat, 1807-1813. Ils portaient un uniforme rouge aux parements bleus, les galons des hommes recrutés étant blanc avec une ligne bleue, à bouts carrés et par deux. Les officiers avaient des boutons et des galons dorés.

C1 Voyageurs canadiens 1812-1815. Les Voyageurs avaient leur propre costume utilitaire. Durant l'été canadien chaud et humide, ils ne portaient parfois qu'une chemise, une culotte et des mocassins. **C2** Voltigeurs canadiens, simple soldat, 1813. Cette unité d'infanterie légère devait être armée de "carabines" et d'accoutrements noirs en 1812. Les carabines étaient tout simplement, semble-t-il, des mousquets de modèle indien équipés d'une baïonnette. **C3** Voltigeur canadien, officier, 1813 qui porte un uniforme vert foncé de style hussard, bordé de noir. Le shako en fourrure semble avoir été adopté à partir de 1812.

D1 Upper Canada Militia, simple soldat, 1813. Beaucoup de miliciens allaient se battre en tenue civile. Le blanc semble avoir été une couleur appréciée pour les badges, car les miliciens du Upper Canada l'utilisèrent de nouveau en 1837-8. **D2** Royal Newfoundland Fencibles, simple soldat, Compagnie de bataillon, 1812-1813. En 1812 et jusqu'en 1813, la plupart des unités régulières en campagne portaient une culotte grise et un shako en tuyau de poêle. **D3** Upper Canada Militia, officier, 2nd Leeds Rifle Company, v. 1812. Aucun uniforme n'était spécifié, mais la veste à courtes basques du Lieutenant Levi Stoper de la Rifle Company of the 2nd Leeds Regiment était verte aux revers noirs, avec des boutons et des galons dorés.

E1 Upper Canada Provincial Artificers, simple soldat, 1813. Cette unité fut sans doute la première au Canada à employer des noirs en service régulier. Son premier uniforme bleu aux revers noirs se serait inspiré de la petite tenue des artificiers militaires royaux. **E2** Upper Canada Militia, simple soldat, 1813. A cause de pénuries de tissu, on distribua des vestes vertes à courtes basques et des culottes bleues début 1813 aux miliciens mobilisés. Des clairons en étain étaient utilisés au lieu de plaques en cuivre sur les shakos. **E3** Canadian Fencibles, tambour, Compagnie de bataillon, 1812-1813. La capote du tambour comportait dix boutonnières galonnées à bout carré, en paires, 26 mètres de galon étroit, et sur les manches, six chevrons à pince dirigés vers le haut.

F1 Lower Canada Sedentary Militia, automne 1813. Ce costume est typique, presqu'entièrement cousu et tissé maison, et est composé d'une cape (généralement grise) avec une ceinture multicolore à la taille, une culotte, de longs mocassins qui ressemblent à des bottes et un calot en laine. **F2** 3rd Battalion Lower Canada Select Embodied Militia, simple soldat, Light Company, 1813. **F3** Canadian Light Dragoons, soldat de cavalerie, 1813 Le capitaine Coleman choisit l'uniforme pratique illustré ici pour ses soldats, qui furent bientôt déployés au Canada Supérieur et qui participèrent à plusieurs engagements.

G1 104th (New Brunswick) Foot, simple soldat, Grenadier Company, 1814-1816. Les épaulettes de la veste à courtes basques ne comportent ni pompons ni franges. Depuis 1800 environ, les grenadiers en service à l'étranger portaient un shako au lieu d'un bonnet à poils. Les plaques 'Belgic' de ce régiment avaient le numéro '104' en-dessous du monogramme. **G2** Upper Canada Militia, officier, 1814 qui porte un uniforme écarlate aux parements bleus, avec des boutons dorés, des manchettes et un col galonnés, un pantalon gris. Les officiers de l'Incorporated Militia portaient un shako, mais pour bien d'autres, le calot rond était standard. **G3** Glengarry Light Infantry, simple soldat, 1812-1816. Cette unité 'écossaise' portait du vert aux parements noirs, comme les 95th Rifles. Ces soldats n'étaient néanmoins pas armés avec des fusils mais avec des mousquets et portaient des accoutrements noirs.

H1 Michigan Fencibles, simple soldat, 1814-1815. Ils avaient une veste rouge à courtes basques et aux parements noirs. Le shako 'Belgic' est illustré, mais les couvre-chefs auraient aussi pu être des 'tuyaux de poêle'. Les mocassins étaient communs. **H2** Indian Department, officier, v. 1813-1815 dans une veste à courtes basques, richement galonnée, sans doute portée avec un bicorne ou, pour les occasions moins formelles, un calot rond. **H3** Western (ou Cadwell's) Rangers, simple soldat, 1813-1815. Ils avaient un uniforme très pratique, composé d'une veste vert uni sans parements, et d'un 'low bucket cap' (un shako tuyau de poêle réduit en hauteur, sans la plaque).

Farbtafeln

A1 Queen's Rangers, Gefreiter, ca. 1797-1802. Dieser Soldat trägt die grüne Jacke, die mit weißen Knopflöchern versehen ist, und den frühen Tschako mit dem Bügelhornabzeichen, der zur damaligen Zeit von mehreren Korps getragen wurde. **A2** King's New Brunswick Regiment, Gefreiter, 1793-1794. Anhand der Aufmachung dieser Einheit werden die Schwierigkeiten ersichtlich, die viele der neu aufgestellten Einheiten in den Kolonien jenseits des Atlantik bei der Beschaffung von Uniformen hatten. **A3** Royal Canadian Volunteers, Gefreiter, 1795-1800. Diese Einheit nahm einige der Änderungen an der Uniform der Infanterieeinheiten nicht vor. Die Mützen waren weiterhin weiß eingefaßt, man trug nach 1797 statt der weißen weiter rote Westen, und die Jacken scheinen bis 1802 Revers gehabt zu haben.

B1 Infanterieoffizier, 1800-1806, im Dienstanzug während des Spätherbst beziehungsweise Ende Frühling. Die runde Mütze mit Pelz-Verzierung blieb bis 1806 in Gebrauch, und die Farbe des Mantels wechselte Ende 1811 von blau zu grau. **B2** Nova Scotia Fencibles, Offizier, 1804-1812. Offizieren der Nova Scotia Fencibles war es ab 1804 gestattet, Tschakos zu tragen. Ansonsten glich ihre Uniform der anderen regulären und Verteidigungs-Regimenter in Britisch-Nordamerika. **B3** 10th Royal Veterans Battalion, Gefreiter, 1807-1813. Die Soldaten trugen rote Uniformen mit blauen Aufschlägen, wobei die Litzen der Mannschaftsgrade weiß mit einer blauen Linie, nicht abgerundet und paarweise angeordnet waren. Die Offiziere trugen Goldknöpfe und -litzen.

C1 Canadian Voyageurs, 1812-1815. Die Voyageurs hatten ihren eigenen, zweckdienlichen Anzug. Während des schwülen kanadischen Sommers trugen sie allerdings oft nur ein Hemd, eine Lendenschurz und Mokassins. **C2** Canadian Voltigeurs, Gefreiter, 1813. Diese Einheit der leichten Infanterie sollte 1812 mit „Karabinern" und schwarzem Zubehör ausgestattet werden, wobei es sich bei den Karabinern offensichtlich einfach um Musketen im indischen Muster mit Bajonetten handelte. **C3** Canadian Voltigeurs, Offizier, 1813. Dieser Offizier trägt eine schwarz eingefaßte, dunkelgrüne Uniform im Husarenstil. Die Pelzmütze scheint ab 1812 in Gebrauch gewesen zu sein.

D1 Upper Canada Militia, Gefreiter, 1813. Viele Milizionäre traten in Zivilkleidung zum Kampf an. Bei Abzeichen scheint die Farbe weiß populär gewesen zu sein, denn 1837-38 kam sie bei den Milizionären des Upper Canada-Regiments erneut zum Einsatz. **D2** Royal Newfoundland Fencibles, Gefreiter der Bataillonskompanie, 1812-1813. Während des Jahres 1812 und noch bis 1813 trugen die meisten regulären Einheiten im Kampf graue Hosen und Ofenrohr-Tschakos. **D3** Upper Canada Militia, Offizier, 2nd Leeds Rifle Company, ca. 1812. Es war keine Uniform vorgegeben, aber der enganliegende kurze Waffenrock von Lt. Levi Soper der Rifle Company des 2nd Leeds Regiment war grün mit schwarzen Aufschlägen und hatte Goldknöpfe und -litzen.

E1 Upper Canada Provincial Artificers, Gefreiter, 1813. Diese Einheit war wahrscheinlich die erste in Kanada, bei der Schwarze regulären Dienst taten. Ihre erste Uniform, die blau mit schwarzem Aufschlägen war, beruhte anscheinend auf der Ausgehuniform der Royal Military Artificers. **E2** Upper Canada Militia, Gefreiter, 1813. Aufgrund von Stoffmangel wurden Anfang 1813 an mobilisierte Milizionäre kurze Waffenröcke in grüner Farbe und blaue Hosen ausgegeben. Auf den Tschakos sah man anstatt der Messingabzeichen Bügelhörner aus Zinn. **E3** Canadian Fencibles, Trommler, Bataillonskompanie, 1812-13. Die Jacke des Trommlers weist zehn paarweise angeordnete Knopflöcher mit eckiger Litzeneinfassung auf sowie 24 Meter schmale Litze. An den Ärmeln waren sechs nach oben zeigende Pfeilwinkel.

F1 Lower Canada Sedentary Militia, Herbst 1813. Die abgebildete Aufmachung ist typischerweise größtenteils selbstgemacht und -genäht. Sie besteht aus einem Soldatenmantel (normalerweise in grauer Farbe) mit einer bunten Schärpe um die Taille, Breeches, langen, stiefelartigen Mokassins und einer Wollmütze. **F2** 3rd Battalion Lower Canada Select Embodied Militia, Gefreiter der leichten Kompanie, 1813 **F3** Canadian Light Dragoons, einfacher Soldat, 1813. Capt. Coleman wählte die hier abgebildete, praktische Uniform für seine Truppe, die schon bald im oberen Kanada zum Einsatz kam und in mehreren Gefechten kämpfte.

G1 104th (New Brunswick) Foot, Gefreiter der Grenadierkompanie, 1814-1816. Die Schulterstücke am Waffenrock hatten keine Quasten oder Fransen. Ab Anfang des 19. Jahrhundert wurden an Grenadiere, die in Übersee Dienst taten, anstelle der Bärenfellmützen Tschakos ausgegeben. Die Tschakoabzeichen der Marke 'Belgic' des Regiments trugen unter dem Monogramm die Ziffer '104'. **G2** Upper Canada Militia, Offizier, 1814. Der Offizier trägt eine scharlachrote Uniform mit blauen Aufschlägen, Goldknöpfen und Litzen an den Manschetten und am Kragen sowie graue Hosen. Offiziere der Incorporated Militia trugen allgemein Tschakos, wohingegen die meisten anderen normalerweise runde Mützen trugen. **G3** Glengarry Light Infantry, Gefreiter, 1812-1816. Diese „schottische" Einheit war wie die 95th Rifles in grün mit schwarzen Aufschlägen gekleidet. Sie waren jedoch nicht mit Gewehren bewaffnet, sondern hatten Musketen und schwarzes Zubehör.

H1 Michigan Fencibles, Gefreiter, 1814-1815. Die Soldaten dieses Regiments trugen kurze rote Waffenröcke mit schwarzen Aufschlägen. Abgebildet ist der Tschako des Typs 'Belgic', doch waren unter Umständen auch 'Ofenrohre' als Kopfbedeckung üblich. Es ist anzunehmen, daß Mokassins gang und gäbe waren. **H2** Indian Department, Offizier, ca. 1813-1815. Dieser Offizier trägt einen kurzen Waffenrock mit aufwendiger Litzenverzierung, der wahrscheinlich mit einem Zweispitz oder bei weniger formellen Anlässen mit einer runden Mütze getragen wurde. **H3** Western (bzw. Cadwell's) Rangers, Gefreiter, 1813-1815. Diese Soldaten trugen eine besonders praktische Uniform, die aus einer einfarbigen grünen Jacke ohne Aufschläge bestand, sowie eine „Kübelmütze", wobei es sich anscheinend um einen verkürzten Ofenrohr-Tschako ohne Abzeichen handelte.